Many years ago, I was teaching an ex
in project management. Every other v
would meet and two of the students h
the best of their ability) an executive-level status report on an existing project. In the first class meeting, two of the students volunteered to "get the pain out of the way" and be first to team up and prepare a status report for the next class meeting.

In the next class meeting, they handed out a 15-page status report to each student. I then followed them around the classroom, picked up all of the status reports, and disposed of them in the trash can while the whole class watched. The two students th`at prepared the reports were quite upset. I then told them to prepare another report for the next class meeting and, if the report had in it a staple or paper clip, I would dispose of it in the same way.

The moral to the story is clear: Executives do not have time to read what's on their desk already, so why give them too much information in which case they will either refuse to read it or study it with a microscope and find a fault. Executives want the answers to two questions: Where are we today? And where will we end up? Do you really believe this cannot be accomplished on a single sheet of paper? The One-Page Project Manager series of books are encouraging you to do just that. Making this part of your Project Management Methodology will simplify and improve your project communication, especially with busy executives.

—Harold D. Kerzner, PhD
Senior Executive Director
International Institute for Learning, Inc.

Clark Campbell fills a void and bridges a communication gap that has long existed between company executives and project or program managers. OPPM successfully links corporate strategy to those in the trenches managing projects."

—Dr. Denis R. Petersen, PMP
President and CEO, Milestone Management Consultants, LLC

Communication may be the single most important critical success factor in project management. I have served as a CIO in 6 high-technology companies over the past 26 years. In this capacity, I have observed many successful, and unsuccessful, projects—including a very successful $30 million SAP/ERP implementation that I participated in using *The One-Page Project Manager.* This tool really works! It makes the complex look simpler, facilitates accurate and honest assessments, and all on just one page—which can, and will be, read by even the busiest executive.

—David C. Berg
Retired Chief Information Officer
IBM, Unisys and Sun Microsystems

If you've ever needed to manage several projects at once, you know the dilemma: there has to be a better way to track the projects quickly, concisely and reliably, but finding and learning that better way always seems too tedious, costly, or complicated. This book solves that problem.

— Frank Luby
Author, *Manage for Profit, not for Market Share*
Harvard Business School Press
Partner, Simon-Kucher & Partners, Strategy and Marketing Consultants

When managing large projects it is easy to lose oneself in gritty details only to wake up and realize that you spent valuable time on the wrong issues. In *The One-Page Project Manager,* Clark Campbell reveals a wonderful tool for keeping projects on task. Only one glance and we see the big issues requiring attention. It's the perfect organizational solution for the executive needing relevant project information.

—Taylor Randall, PhD
Professor, David Eccles School of Business
University of Utah

While at initial glance this book may appear to be simply about developing a "dashboard" for tracking an important project, it soon becomes clear that it is much more than that. The approach outlined by Clark Campbell, an experienced and accomplished project leader, provides a proven process for project management that significantly improves the chances that the project will be completed on time, on budget, and on target for its intended purposes. Furthermore, it provides a straightforward yet compelling set of steps to ensure that those with the ability and responsibility to achieve the desired results are supported, guided, and focused in their efforts to do so. This approach will prove especially beneficial to students and practitioners who want to learn and apply the skills and tools of effective project leadership.

—Steven C. Wheelwright, PhD
Baker Foundation Professor
Senior Associate Dean
Director of Publications Activities
Harvard Business School
Harvard University

This is the most productive method I've seen to capture the essence of project management. Not too complicated, not too simple. For those with experience this is certainly a method to adopt for rapid, vivid, and persistent communication. I wish I'd had this years ago, but am glad it came along now. It clearly saves time for an organization's key resources.

— Paul Germeraad, PhD
President of Intellectual Assets, Inc.
Instructor, Caltech

Impressive in its simplicity, yet universal in its application, the *One-Page Project Manager* began assisting Chinese project managers in 2003, when Mr. Campbell first lectured in Beijing. OPPM is easy to learn and use, and is impressive in its clear capacity to communicate. It should be required reading for every manager who wants to improve project performance, accurately tell their story, and do it efficiently.

— Jonathan H. Du, PhD
CEO and Chairman
WiseChina Training Ltd.
Beijing, China

Total Lean Management requires lean communication. Clark Campbell and Mike Collins have presented in this book a powerfully simple communication tool. O.C. Tanner, a Shingo Prize winner, is among the top 3% of Lean companies in North America. Their distinctive combination of OPPM with Toyota's A3 report reveals a unique continuous improvement, one which documents, in part, how they have executed their strategy to achieve market dominance and profitable growth.

—Ross E. Robson, PhD
Strategic Founder and Executive
Director of the Shingo Prize (retired),
and President, DnR Lean LLC

THE ONE-PAGE PROJECT MANAGER FOR EXECUTION

DRIVE STRATEGY & SOLVE PROBLEMS WITH A SINGLE SHEET OF PAPER

CLARK A. CAMPBELL
WITH
MIKE COLLINS

John Wiley & Sons, Inc.

Published by John Wiley & Sons, Inc., Hoboken, New Jersey.

Published simultaneously in Canada.

For general information on our other products and services or for technical support, please contact our Customer Care Department within the United States at (800) 762-2974, outside the United States at (317) 572-3993 or fax (317) 572-4002.

Wiley also publishes its books in a variety of electronic formats. Some content that appears in print may not be available in electronic books. For more information about Wiley products, visit our web site at www.wiley.com.

ISBN: 978-0470-49933-7

Printed in the United States of America

10 9 8 7 6 5 4 3 2 1

CONTENTS

FIGURES

Clark Campbell has been my friend and colleague for over 20 years. We met on the soccer sideline watching, then driving, then coaching our kids through this phase of our lives. As I spent significant parts of 11 Thanksgiving vacations on long, soccer-related road trips with Clark, I came to appreciate his analytic mind and his incessant search for better ways to run things generally and projects specifically.

One day I accepted his invitation to observe the status of a new facility he was directing. It was my first acquaintance with the one-page project manager (OPPM). My first exposure to OPPM was a private tutorial from Clark Campbell. He was rightfully enthusiastic, and I was sincerely impressed with the elegant simplicity, breadth, and capacity of this one-page system. Given our history, it did not surprise me that Clark had found a better way to track, trace, and create accountability.

Simultaneous with the development of OPPM, I entered government service. I ultimately joined Governor Mike Leavitt, a three-term governor of Utah, as his chief of staff, first in his governor's office, then as he became administrator of the U.S. Environmental Protection Agency, and finally as he served as secretary of the U.S. Department of Health and Human Services (HHS). A few metrics are helpful in explaining the size and scope of HHS. With over 67,000 employees and a federal budget exceeding $700 billion, HHS would rank as the 4th or 5th largest economy in the world.

A chief of staff is, in part, a COO, a problem solver, and the implementer of his boss's agenda and priorities. At each new venue Mike Leavitt and I created a document of our vision (a 500-day plan with a 5,000-day horizon), out of which typically grew immense, expansive projects. Our application of basic project planning into our large strategic government policy initiatives was, I think, unique.

As an example, the projects at HHS included national and international preparedness for pandemic influenza. This included a preparedness summit in each state, the reintroduction of the vaccine industry in the United States, and efforts to encourage personal, business, institutional, and governmental preparedness. We organized the Value Driven Health Care initiative, created a national collaboration for health information technology, drove public and global health initiatives, organized a personalized medicine initiative, and pushed the ethic of prevention.

Each of these was a huge national or international undertaking. Each was dynamic and continually evolving. Each required remarkable collaborative planning and execution. For each of these HHS projects we chose the OPPM as an integral tool to reflect our status, identify barriers, determine next steps, and make necessary adjustments. Through our monthly report utilizing OPPM I was updated clearly and effectively on each of these initiatives. Armed with my OPPM, my monthly report to the secretary was made immeasurably easier, more straightforward, and more accurate.

Our execution with OPPM was far from perfect, but our outcomes, our communication, our capacity for thoughtful deliberation, and our ability to make adjustments were significantly improved by so effectively consolidating large amounts of information in a concise and easy-to-translate way.

I can imagine larger projects than those that we engaged in, but not a place where there would be 11 of such magnitude going simultaneously. I can't imagine trying to keep track of all of it without the proper tools, and for us the OPPM was a key component. It is great to know that there is an organizational genius like Clark Campbell among us. Simply stated, our use of OPPM helped us keep a lot of things airborne and on target.

I suppose a postscript of sorts is in order. After 16 years in public service, in the case of Secretary Leavitt, and 12 for me, we started Leavitt Partners, where we advise and invest in companies that we think are positioning themselves for the world we hope to see. A key part of each client relationship is the development of an OPPM.

—RICH MCKEOWN
President and CEO
Leavitt Partners, LLC

Throughout my 30 years of operations and leadership experience, I have sought out philosophies and tools that could advance my organizations. Quality circles, just-in-time, statistical process control, Six Sigma, Lean, and many more practices have made their impacts with varying degrees of success.

I now realize an important principle: the more people involved in problem solving and process improvement, the faster the progress. Although we have learned to use many of the Lean tools at O.C. Tanner Co., it seems to me that simple tools can be the most useful means for helping every person contribute.

The difficulty has been that project-management disciplines have not been simple. Some might say that only professional project managers, engineers, and upper management can plan and implement a project. They might believe that project management is a complicated discipline not easily taught to people on the floor.

Given its ease of use and understandable structure, *The One-Page Project Manager* is a welcome solution to this complexity. We train managers and team members to use it. It has enabled people on the floor to manage their own *kaizen* projects. They have applied its project disciplines and simple communication capabilities to plan schedules, meet objectives, define responsibility, manage work, and report status. With it in our Lean tool kit, we have tapped into the creativity of our people to pump up productivity, cut cycle times, slash work in process (WIP), trim floor space, deliver on time better than ever, and drive product and service quality to be world-class.

In *The One-Page Project Manager for Execution,* Clark Campbell and Mike Collins present how OPPM works in conjunction with strategy deployment. They illustrate use of A3s and OPPMs to document how projects align to a strategic vision. These tools work together to make sure a strategy is clearly understood throughout an organization, and that the progress of supporting projects can be monitored easily.

With our emphasis on building a culture of continuous improvement and respect for people, OPPM has become a simple but invaluable tool for our people as they refine and strengthen our business. Enjoy the book and empower your people to use it!

—Harold Simons
Executive Vice President, Supply Chain,
O.C. Tanner Company
Member of the Shingo Prize Board of Governors
Recipient of the Shingo Prize for
Manufacturing Excellence, 1999

ACKNOWLEDGMENTS

To our associates at the O.C. Tanner Company and the American Shizuki Corporation, who, together with their leaders, provided the learning laboratory from which the thoughts and simple methods articulated in this book emerged, evolved, were verified, and then were extended to other organizations.

To the astute team at John Wiley & Sons, Inc., including Shannon Vargo, Beth Zipko, and Deborah Schindlar, who executed this book project with diligence and wisdom.

Special appreciation is extended to Kent Murdock, whose vision and encouragement made this and the other OPPM books possible, and to Yasuhiko Kajikawa, a personal mentor and leading sensei of lean thinking.

CLARK A. CAMPBELL
MICHAEL J. COLLINS

INTRODUCTION

In my first two books, *The One-Page Project Manager* and *The One-Page Project Manager for IT Projects*, I covered in detail the thinking behind this valuable tool for project managers and how to construct one. In this book, I, together with Mike Collins, will expand the audience to include executives and leaders responsible for executing strategy. We will discuss how to add OPPM™ to the Toyota one-page A3 report and give specific examples of how these communication tools help drive strategy and solve problems in a remarkably simple way.

The one-page project manager (or OPPM) was developed in the early 1990s at the O.C. Tanner Company in Salt Lake City, Utah. It was first used in a $10 million construction and computer system project to build an automated distribution center and then on a growing number of projects over more than a decade. By 1997, Mike Collins joined the Tanner team, bringing with him his 20 years of experience with the Toyota production system. I would call Mike a Lean expert, yet he would say he is still simply a student. Mike was vice president and general manager of the American Shizuki Corporation, moved on to WorldTech Consulting in Southeast Asia, and now, in addition to his appointment as vice president of Lean enterprise development for

O.C. Tanner, he continues to teach graduate courses on Lean principles at Westminster College.

It was Mike who first suggested that OPPM would be a powerful visual tool to efficiently communicate all the information contained on the right side of the one-page Toyota A3 report. Mike has put his idea to work with hundreds of problem-solving projects over the past 10 years. It was the success (unexpected even to Mike) of his work using OPPM and A3 to solve problems and drive strategy that provided the impetus for this book. People in manufacturing, and more recently across the enterprise, were executing the strategy because they were both conversant with and aligned to their required elements. OPPM and A3 communicated the right information to the right people at the right time to not only monitor, but to reinforce and reward getting the right things done — yes, execution!

THE KEY:

Execution, with simple communication.

Sun Tzu would say, "good execution is the foundation of good strategy, and great execution increases strategic options." (See *Sun Tzu for Execution*, by Steven W. Michaelson.) And even more simply stated, "Strategies most often fail because they aren't executed well." See Execution by Larry Bossidy and Ram Charan.

Edward Tufte is professor emeritus at Yale University, where he taught courses in statistical evidence and information design. In his remarkable book, *The Visual*

Display of Quantitative Information, he says, "Often the most effective way to describe, explore, and summarize a set of numbers—even a very large set—is to look at pictures of those numbers. Furthermore, of all methods for analyzing and communicating statistical information, well-designed data graphics are usually the simplest and at the same time the most powerful."

Einstein is reputed to have said, "Everything should be made as simple as possible, but no simpler."

THE GUIDING PRINCIPLE:

Be as simple as is practicable.

Practicable is precisely the right word here. Not just as simple as possible, but as simple as practicable. Practicable has roots in Medieval Latin (practicabilis—capable of being used) and Greek (praktikos—fit for action). Synonyms would include achievable, attainable, feasible, *executable.*

Peter Drucker reminds us that "Management by Objectives works—if you know the objectives. Unfortunately, 90 percent of the time you don't." OPPM™/A3s secure a project to a strategic purpose, plan the critical elements, and then easily communicate performance of the key variables.

THE PROCESS:

Communication

Finally, before we launch into the specifics of OPPM and A3s, a word about communication. I have had the privilege to travel and speak together with two other authors in the "Three Nationally Renowned Best Selling Authors in the Project Management" series sponsored by the Project Management Resource Group. Michael J. Cunningham, president and founder of the Harvard Computing Group, writes in his book, *Finish What You Start*, "One of the most complex issues about larger-scale project management is *visualizing* what is happening. *Communication* may be time consuming and might not appear to produce immediate results, but trust me, this *is the big one.*" Andy Crowe, author of *Alpha Project Managers: What the Top 2% Know that Everyone Else Does Not,* says, "Of all the attributes that separate the Alpha group from their peers, *communication presents the most striking difference.*"

This book has been written to stand on its own without referring back to the previous two OPPM books. To that end, we have revised, refined, and included material from the other books.

Chapter 1 explains the links and ties of OPPM to strategy. With a little personal history, you will see how OPPM, first designed as a simple project management tool, found its way into Lean practices, Toyota methods, and finally strategy deployment.

While presenting the essential elements of the first OPPM book to a Board of Directors, one board member wryly asked if I had a "one-page version" of the book.

Chapter 2 is an attempt to summarize that first book. You will see how to construct and report using the OPPM and be given a few tips to ensure it gets used. OPPMs can be used alone or in conjunction with a Toyota A3 report to both drive strategy and solve problems. It has been said, "a problem is a project in disguise." Chapter 3 provides specific examples of how OPPM was used to help plan, staff, direct, control, and communicate a project to secure ISO certification.

Chapter 4 introduces the Toyota A3 report with its connections to scientific method and Deming's Plan-Do-Check-Act cycle. We will then reexamine the ISO example in Chapter 5, bringing OPPM into the A3 report.

The project management office is essential to Lean execution. Chapter 6 discusses how OPPM supports the eight fundamental responsibilities of your PMO. We share with you the Project Office Template, or OPPM, which summarizes the top-priority projects and links them to both strategy and annual operating plans.

Chapter 7 brings the power and simplicity of A3 into the strategy deployment process. You will see actual examples of the OPPM/A3 cascades from the corporate level out through the business-function level to the team level.

We move beyond strategy to solving specific problems using OPPM/A3 in Chapter 8. You will see how these tools facilitate continuous improvement and how they amplify the "respect for people," requirement of the Toyota business system.

Because OPPM and A3 are so simple and so visual, a few thoughts from the experts would be appropriate to conclude this introduction.

> "At every step we've noted the need for managers to see . . . to bring perfection into *clear view* so the objective of improvement is *visible* and real."
>
> "Lean thinking is a series of *simple* but counterintuitive ideas. . . ."
>
> —JAMES P. WOMACK & DANIEL T. JONES
> Authors of *Lean Thinking*, and the first to use the word "Lean"

> "The most time-consuming and difficult way to understand complex ideas is to have to decipher a lengthy report . . . more efficient is the visual approach . . . people are visually oriented, new employees at Toyota learn to communicate with as few words as possible and with visual aids. The A3 report is a key part of the process."
>
> —JEFFREY K. LIKER
> Author of *The Toyota Way*

> "Our purpose is to outline a simple system for implanting PDCA management—a system that is simple yet disciplined and rigorous. It centers on the use of what Toyota terms A3 reports —one page documents that record the main results from the PDCA cycle."
>
> —DURWARD K. SOBEK II, & ART SMALLEY
> Authors of *Understanding A3 Thinking*

"But complex things create order too, the way the cogs and springs and flywheels of a watch yield a single, simple piece of data —the time—and that piece of data in turn runs the world."

"There is a taxonomy of things that fool us every day and, in so doing, help the complex masquerade as the simple, and the simple parade itself as complex."

—Jeffrey Kluger

Author of *Simplexity: Why Simple Things Become Complex (and How Complex Things Can Be Made Simple)*

"New science is also making us more aware that our yearning for simplicity is one we share with natural systems."

—Margaret J. Wheatley

Author of *Leadership and the New Science*

"It seems that perfection is reached not when there is nothing left to add, but when there is nothing left to take away."

—Antoine de Saint Exupery

"Simplicity is the ultimate sophistication."

—Leonardo da Vinci

"I would not give a fig for the simplicity this side of complexity, but I would give my life for the simplicity on the other side of complexity."

—Attributed to Oliver Wendell Holmes, Jr.

CHAPTER

OPPM and Strategy Execution

Two retired CEOs, friends for over three decades, exchanged memories about their business experiences. One was previously managing partner of the biggest private real estate firm in the country and was now chairman of a successful airline. The other had, for 12 years, directed O.C. Tanner, the 80-year-old global leader in recognition and appreciation. This time they spoke of ideas and tools that had made their work easier and more effective. What really made a difference? One comment resounded with the usual candor and clarity that always accompanied their conversations. "OPPM was simple, yet it was the single most valuable tool I used to execute the strategy and get the right things done," insisted Kent Murdock, retired Tanner CEO. Those "right things" included lifting sales, increasing profits, and enlarging stockholder return to the highest levels in company history. Joel Peterson, current chairman of JetBlue and faculty member at Stanford's Graduate School of Business, added that "if OPPM could communicate strategy simply, and could align execution of that strategy to people, processes, and performance metrics, on a single sheet of paper, it should be in every CEO's toolkit."

In their #1 *New York Times* bestseller *Execution, The Discipline of Getting Things Done*, Larry Bossidy and Ram Charan said:

> *Along with having clear goals, you should strive for simplicity in general. One thing you'll notice about leaders who execute is that they speak simply and directly. They talk plainly and forthrightly about what's on their minds. They know how to simplify things so that others can understand them, evaluate them, and act on them, so that what they say becomes common sense.*

Bossidy and Charan teach that execution is a "discipline for meshing strategy with reality, aligning people with goals, and achieving the results promised . . . linking the people process, the strategy, and the operating plan together to get things done on time."

HOW DID THE ONE-PAGE PROJECT MANAGER (OPPM), A TOOL DEVELOPED FOR PROJECT MANAGEMENT, GET TANGLED UP WITH STRATEGY?

Clark relates the following about the coming together of the one-page project manager (OPPM™) and

Lean—how OPPM found its way into strategy deployment through pursuit of the Shingo Prize:

The sun broke fully from behind the disappearing clouds, unseasonably warming the winter morning in Salt Lake City, Utah. My wife Meredith and I observed as the families of the bride and groom were escorted, following the ceremony, into planned poses by an experienced and demanding photographer. The daughter of close friends from our college years was the happiest of brides, beautiful and basking in every moment of this, her day.

Meredith's attention was drawn to the sister of the bride, mine to her uncle. The rest of the story is about execution (getting things done) and therefore a most fitting beginning to this, the third book in the OPPM series.

Uncle Stephen M. Beckstead, PhD, associate director of the Shingo Prize for Excellence in Manufacturing, had traveled in for the wedding. We at O.C. Tanner Company were striving to meet the Shingo standards and win the prize. Time between the various photo set-ups provided an opportunity to visit with Steve, and open discussions concerning our readiness for an application.

Quality had always been a passion of Obert Tanner, founder, in 1927, of the company that carries his name. We organized a formal quality department in 1980 and hired outside consultants, for the first time, to help us with metrics and proven processes. I became vice president for quality in 1996, and in addition to the work of our department, observed the efforts of Harold Simons, executive vice president of manufacturing, to incorporate Lean principles and practices into the manufacturing operations.

It was January 2, 1999, as Dr. Beckstead and I visited between wedding pictures. O.C. Tanner had been attempting for several years to eliminate manufacturing waste, to apply portions of the Toyota Production System, and to imbed Lean principles and practices into our operations. We certainly had come a long way, but was it far enough? Was now the time to apply?

After sets of probing questions, Steve agreed to visit our plant for a high-level assessment. Immediately following his visit and encouraging conclusions, I decided the Tanner Company should apply for the Shingo Prize. Harold was skeptical, knowing that much work still needed to be done. Moreover, our marketing leader worried that our then current level of quality problems, although measurably less than our competition, would preclude us from winning the prize. Senior management, however, gave me the go-ahead to apply.

As a member of our operating committee, I approached my peers across the firm, asking for team members to complete the substantial application. With departments already running beyond capacity, coupled with an absence of confidence that we were yet good enough, no operating leader was willing to deploy the quality of talent necessary to tackle the arduous task that lay before us, especially given a short lead time prior to the application deadline.

What happened next should not have been surprising to us. We extended a general invitation for volunteers to anyone who would be interested in working on our Shingo application. We advised them that it would be a project taking about a month, and the team would begin working each evening at 5:00 PM and go until midnight! The response was most encouraging. A full team comprised of all the necessary skills just happened to show up.

Together, we collected the data, going back over the years of effort and results, and completed the required application. Following their meticulous review of the application, a team of three Shingo examiners were deployed for a comprehensive site visit, verification, and analysis. Several weeks later, the Tanner Company was notified that, indeed, we had successfully "challenged" and were awarded the Shingo Prize for Excellence in Manufacturing.

Following the receipt of the prize, I accepted a position on the Shingo board of governors. After completing my term of service on the board, Harold Simons filled my spot, where, as of this writing, he continues to add a depth of experience as not only a student of Lean, but as one who has merged the Toyota Production System with Lean thinking, OPPM, and A3 reports. He passionately drives Lean practices in manufacturing and advances their adoption throughout the entire enterprise.

Harold directed 4 members of his staff to, in addition to managing Lean efforts at Tanner, become scrupulously trained and then volunteer as Shingo examiners themselves.

Now before we move on, how did Meredith do in her efforts to secure results? She found her way to the sister of the bride and suggested that it might be well for Jenny to date our son Jarv. Over the mild objections of her siblings, Jenny and Jarv did call each other, even though they were attending universities in two different cities. And speaking of getting things done, they were engaged three months later, married four months after that, and now, at the time of this writing, have happily welcomed their fourth child into their cheerful family.

O.C. Tanner Company was now conversant with and committed to Lean. Kent, however, was vigilant in reminding us of the pitfalls associated with an obsessive devotion to a single business "doctrine." He demanded that we "wrestle it through" until we found the right balance and right fit for each set of ideas.

An almost unavoidable, certainly natural confluence of events seemed to thrust OPPM toward the execution of strategy. The tool promotes and supports Lean thinking and is itself Lean, pushing so much of the waste (or muda, as Toyota would say) out of the project communication process that it became an integral part of O. C. Tanner Company's continued Lean pursuits and our efforts to use the right mix of strategic principles. This included incorporating and aligning OPPM with our iterations of Dr. Robert S. Kaplan's Strategy Map and its accompanying Balanced Scorecard.

While Mike and I both labored with these powerful ideas at our firm, Mike continued to teach Lean principles to his evening university students, and I found myself traveling and speaking more frequently on OPPM.

As previously mentioned, Mike was the first to recognize how OPPM fit into Toyota's Lean, single-page A3 report. He incorporated it and drove hundreds of problem-solving projects, some small and some rather large, using OPPM/A3s. Together, we designed our balanced scorecard, linked it to the corporate strategy map, and aligned it, through our project-management office, to the prioritization of corporate projects and their subsequent performance metrics. A certain clarity emerged. Every employee was more conversant with, committed to, and engaged in getting the right things done. Strategy was being executed.

While this was incubating at our firm, hundreds of thousands of OPPM templates were downloaded from www.onepageprojectmanager.com to individuals, firms, and even governments across the globe. From a university president requiring OPPMs for every project coming across his desk to a mother planning her daughter's wedding. From a CEO in Beijing, China to a project manager in Madrid, Spain. From a managing partner of a giant consulting firm in Boston to a boomer mom in Saratoga, California. From a program manager in Abu

Dhabi to the U.S. government, which has used the system extensively in pandemic planning and the tracking of the globalization of the FDA, with offices in China, India, Latin America, and Europe.

We will now try to share with you, in this short book, examples of how you can use OPPM and A3 to drive strategy and solve problems—indeed, how these tools will help you simplify Lean improvements and communicate essential elements of the Toyota Production System on a single sheet of paper. We will show you a proven path to engage your team to execute your strategy.

CHAPTER

What Is an OPPM?

First we want to cover, in an abbreviated form, how to construct an OPPM. If you have read the first OPPM book, this chapter, which is based on that book, will provide a useful review. If you have not read that book, this will give you the basics so you can start applying the tool in your everyday work life.

THE THINKING BEHIND THE OPPM

Imagine your boss asking you to quickly provide a report on your project: What aspects of the project are on, ahead, or behind schedule? Who is responsible for each of the project's major tasks? How is the project performing in terms of the budget? How well is the project meeting its objectives? What major problems have cropped up? Generally, how well is the project presently progressing, and what is forecast for the next three months?

Wow, you think, that's a major undertaking. It will take me and my team hours to collect and organize that much information and put it into a presentable form.

This could hurt our performance because this is time away from directly working on the project. And then there's a good chance the boss won't even read all of it because things are always hectic and the boss is always very, very busy.

After working on enough projects, we knew it was a challenge to provide upper management with the information it needed about a project, to provide it in a way that was easily understood and digested, and to collect and present the information in a format that did not take up too much of our time or our team's.

This was the impetus behind the creation of the OPPM. The promise of this tool: It will convey all the salient information a project's stakeholders need to know and provide it in a timely, easy-to-understand, and easy-to-compile format. The OPPM is a communication tool unlike any other available to the project manager. It is designed primarily to communicate aspects of a project to those who are not part of the project, both inside and outside the organization.

Every project has a constituency deeply interested, though not directly involved in it, yet few project managers know how to effectively communicate with this constituency.

This constituency includes the board of directors, senior management, suppliers, customers, superiors or subordinates indirectly involved with the project or its outcome, and others. They want to be told what is going on in ways that engage them and doesn't waste their time, but they don't want to be given long reports with very detailed analyses. Yet, they also don't want communications that are too brief, too inconsequential, or too unsubstantial. These tend to generate more questions than they answer. Instead, they want enough information to answer their questions, but not so much information as to cause them to become inundated with facts and figures.

The OPPM neatly balances their need to know with their desire to know just enough in a format that is easy to read. It answers more questions than it generates, which is why it is such an effective communication tool.

VISUAL ASPECTS OF THE OPPM

The OPPM uses symbols and color to paint a visual, easy-to-understand picture of where a project is at any given moment in time. And it links important components of a project. For example, managers of each part of a project are linked to their part in terms of deadlines and challenges. Senior management immediately sees who is responsible for what and how well each part of the project is going. Outstanding performance that exceeds the plan shows up, and both management and peers immediately know who is personally responsible and who should be recognized.

An aspect of a project that is going well is illustrated with a bright green box or filled-in dot. An aspect behind in terms of time or over budget is highlighted in bright red. When there is ambiguity, yellow is used. This use of color makes the OPPM visually clear and informative and allows senior management to quickly see what is going well, what is in trouble, and where there are some questions.

The layout of the OPPM also visually helps clarify the tool's information. Timelines, lines of responsibility, budget, tasks, and objectives are interrelated on the OPPM—just as they are in real life. The reader can quickly make connections between the important aspects of a project because of how the tool is graphically designed.

Let us here make a statement that may at first seem counterintuitive. Efficient, effective project management has just the right amount of details, while it avoids too many. Often, the more detailed and more elegant a plan is, the more pedantic and plodding the execution becomes. The details can become the drivers, and when this happens, you lose sight of what's important and the management process becomes ineffective. Eventually the project breaks down and fails. Again, things should be as simple as practicable.

One of the strengths of the OPPM—which is where it can be counterintuitive—is having just the right degree of the *absence of precision*. For example, those deeply immersed in a project will want to know the status of critical equipment for a project, for example, if it has been manufactured, if it has been shipped, and where is it now. But management only wants to know if it will arrive on time. The details of what it will take to make sure that critical equipment arrives on time are beyond the interests of management. They don't need to know that. This is an example of what we mean when we say the OPPM has an absence of precision; it doesn't cover every detail, nor should it.

Before we go into the specific steps involved in creating an OPPM, let us clarify one of its great strengths. It is a communication tool that can be used for almost every type of project. It may need to be tweaked when applied to different projects, but the basic skin and bones of the tool remain surprisingly consistent. When paired with Toyota's A3 report, an OPPM can drive strategy and serve as a powerful tool for solving problems, as we will discuss later in this book. At O.C. Tanner in Salt Lake City, Utah, we've used these two combined reports in conjunction with our strategy map and Balanced Scorecard©. We learned that OPPM worked for general projects, IT projects, and, in a most helpful way, for strategy deployment when coupled with our A3s.

The One-Page Project Manager navigates between failing to plan and over-planning. The plan is just the beginning, the means to the end, but not the end.

All of a project's owners are readily identifiable to everyone with the One-Page Project Manager. Owners have no place to hide when a project is being monitored with this tool.

It makes clear—visually, through the use of interconnected graphics and color—who is responsible for what and how they are performing. Senior management sees immediately, by glancing at one page, who is performing well and who is behind on their portion of the project.

Not only does this visualization make it easier for management to understand a project's status and who is responsible, but it is also an important motivator to the owners. They know that their role and performance is continually and immediately visible to senior management.

THE FIVE ESSENTIAL PARTS OF A PROJECT AND THE OPPM

The One-Page Project Manager doesn't replace your existing tools; it augments what you are already using.

The information presented isn't new. What's new is that existing information is placed in a format that is easy to use and to read. That's not a trivial distinction. By placing information in a new, easy-to-grasp format, management becomes better informed and those involved with the project become more highly motivated.

Every project has five essential elements (see Figure 2.1). It is not coincidental that the OPPM also has the same five elements; we have used the elements that make up all projects as the structure on which we build the OPPM. These elements are part of a project manager's DNA. They are second nature. The five elements are:

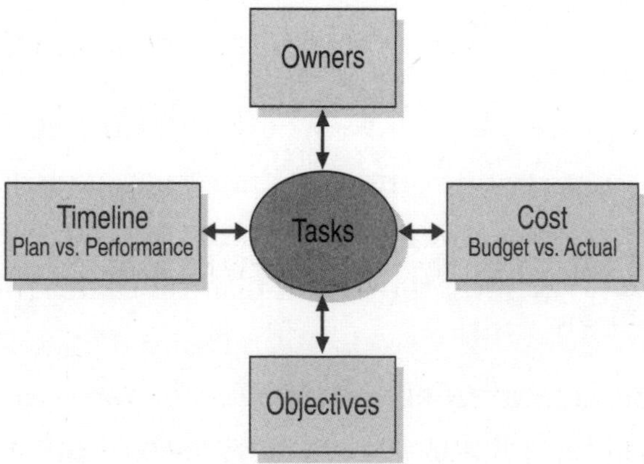

FIGURE 2.1 *Five Essential Elements of Every Project*

1. *Tasks: The how*—Tasks are the center of a project and need to be done to accomplish the objectives. They are the nuts and bolts of a project, the specifics of what needs to be done—the work.
2. *Objectives: The what and the why*—Objectives are the vision, the where-you-are-going of a project. Objectives can be general or specific—the scope.
3. *Timeline: The when*—The timeline measures when things are supposed to be done and when they are actually done. Timelines can be elastic. If a project is expanded, for example, the timeline (and the budget) will probably have to be expanded.
4. *Cost: The how much*—Project expenses can have *hard* costs—such as consulting or machinery—or *soft* costs—such as internal staff deployed on the project. Cost accounting can be complex, and every project needs input from accounting professionals.
5. *Owners: The who*—Task owners are the "who". This is vital. The OPPM makes clear to management who owns what tasks. Clear ownership makes obvious who deserves commendations for jobs well done and who needs to be assisted.

THE 12 STEPS TO CONSTRUCTING THE OPPM

The project's manager and the project's owners together build and maintain the OPPM, and then they live with it. Creating the OPPM and updating it must be a team effort.

Owners own it. You, as the project manager, may have to negotiate with team members, but ultimately you need their buy-in and full commitment. Let's now look at the 12 steps needed to create an OPPM (see Figure 2.2).

Step 1: The Header

This goes at the top of the form and includes the project's name, project leader, project objective, and project current date (see Figure 2.3).

Naming a project is important, because the name is what everyone will use to refer to the project from now

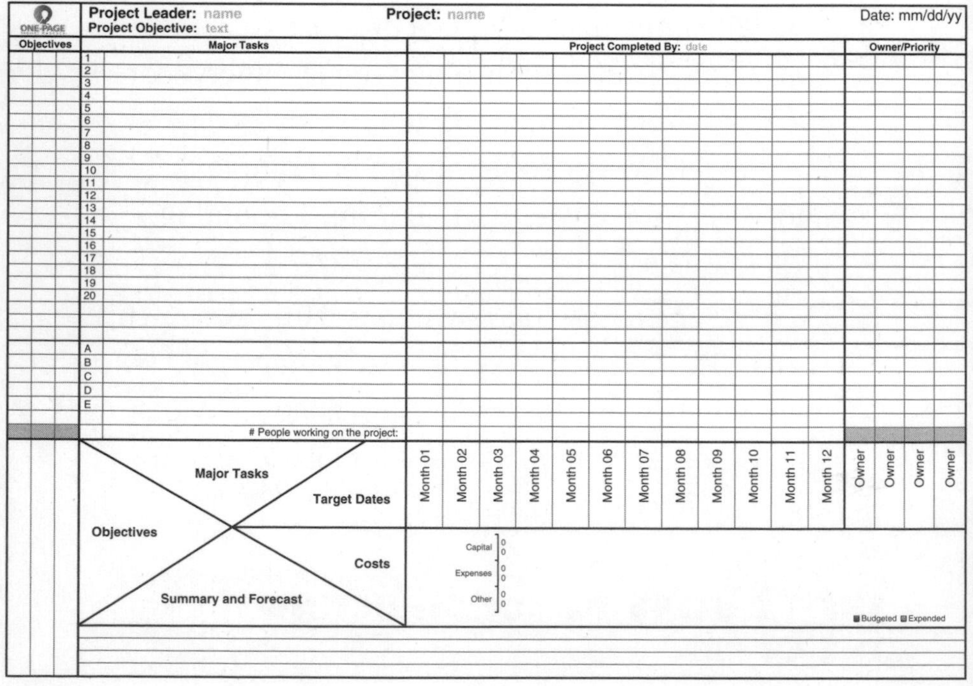

FIGURE 2.2 *Standard Template*

 To customize this document, download it to your hard drive from the following web site: www.oppmi.com. The document can be opened, edited, and printed using Microsoft Excel or another popular spreadsheet application.

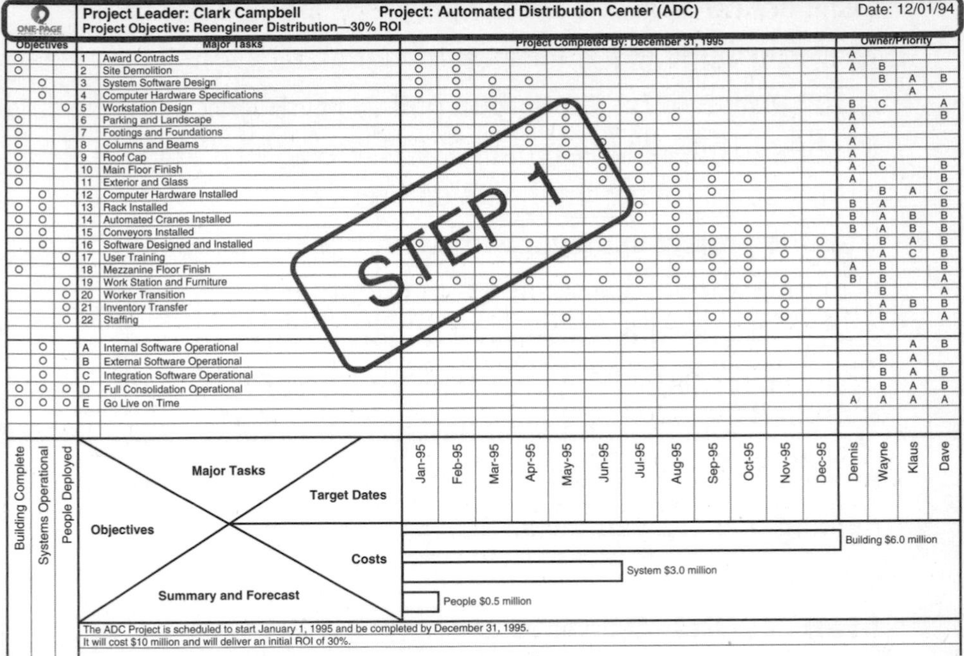

FIGURE 2.3 *The 12 Construction Steps—Step 1*

 To customize this document, download it to your hard drive from the following web site: www.oppmi.com. The document can be opened, edited, and printed using Microsoft Excel or another popular spreadsheet application.

until the project is finished and even beyond. Consider holding off naming the project until the team is in place.

The project leader is the ultimate owner, and every project requires one, but only one. This person is almost invariably a full-time employee of the company, not a consultant or outside advisor.

The project objective is usually given to the project manager by the same people who gave him or her the project in the first place. If the project manager has not been given an objective, he or she must go back to those who assigned the project and clarify the objective. The objective should make clear why those who assigned the project want the project to be done and what they hope to gain from the project.

The preliminary completion date is established at this time. Through the remaining 11 steps, the team's commitment to that final date emerges.

As the project manager works through the header with the executive assigning him the project, it is a good time to discuss the priorities of the project's triple constraints of costs, scope, and timeline. The project manager will be making tradeoff decisions throughout the project. The key guiding principle will be management's ranking of these variables.

Step 2: The Owners

We'll assume from this point on that you are the project manager. Your next step is to name your team. These are the people who will manage the major components of the project. Your success, to a large degree, depends on them. They are the owners. Keep the number of owners as small as possible. From our experience, three or four is usually about right (see Figure 2.4). On a large project, there will be more than one layer of OPPMs, and each will have its own set of owners.

Step 3: The Matrix—The Tool's Foundation

Think of the matrix as the focal point, the hub of the project as expressed on the OPPM (see Figure 2.5). To use a metaphor, think of the matrix as a compass that

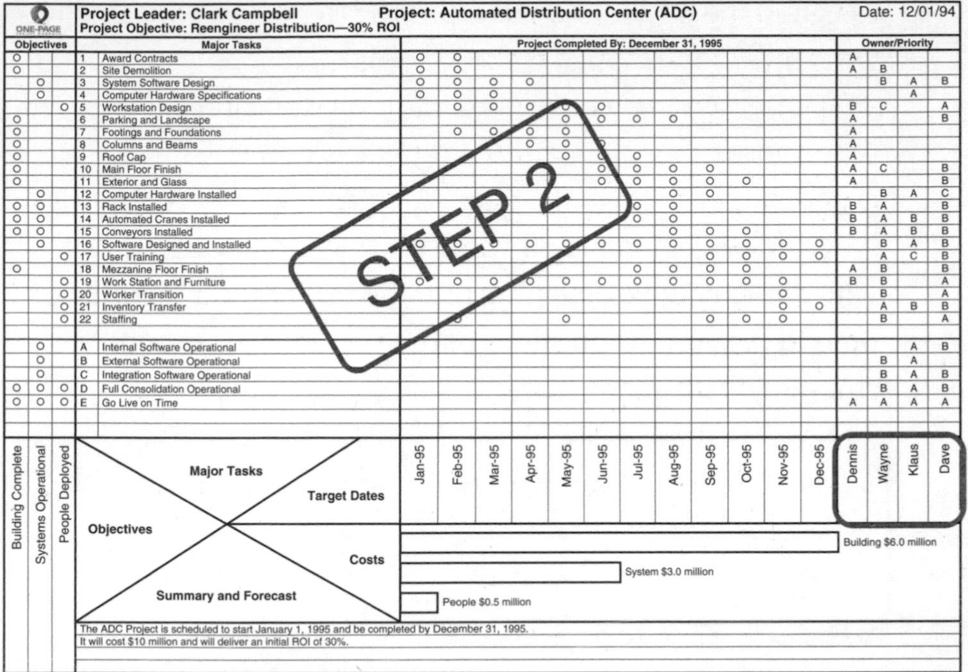

FIGURE 2.4 *The 12 Construction Steps—Step 2*

 To customize this document, download it to your hard drive from the following web site: www.oppmi.com. The document can be opened, edited, and printed using Microsoft Excel or another popular spreadsheet application.

will guide your project from start to finish. The matrix is the OPPM's foundation. It links all of a project's essential elements and communicates them to your readers.

The matrix flows naturally out of the creation of the entire OPPM. During this step, as project manager, you will want to present to your team an overview of the project, discuss how to handle the project, and thoroughly go through the pieces of the matrix, including objectives, major project tasks, target dates, and budget. The matrix is the focal point around which you will teach your team the fundamentals of the OPPM. You

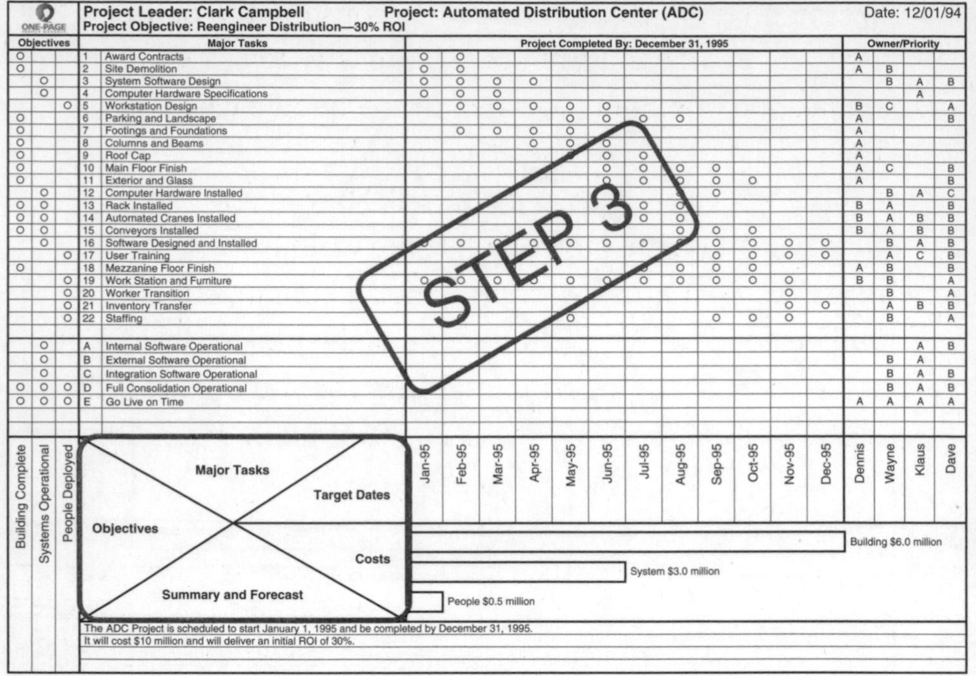

FIGURE 2.5 *The 12 Construction Steps—Step 3*

 To customize this document, download it to your hard drive from the following web site: www.oppmi.com. The document can be opened, edited, and printed using Microsoft Excel or another popular spreadsheet application.

may be surprised by the apparent need for you to teach some of the basics of project management to your team.

Step 4: Project Objectives

With your team in place, you are now ready to break down the project into second-level objectives required to meet the main objective delineated in the header. Objectives go in the rectangle on the lower left-hand corner of the OPPM. Have no more than three or four objectives. For a $10 million distribution center project, we had three objectives: complete construction of the building; have the distribution center's systems operational; and hire, train, and deploy the people who will be running the center (see Figure 2.6).

To set up objectives, ask yourself: How much time will be needed to complete the various objectives? What resources (financial, human, etc.) will be needed? What is the scope of the project (scope refers to the final deliverables)? Later, as you outline the tasks, you will want a fairly equal distribution of tasks for each second-level objective.

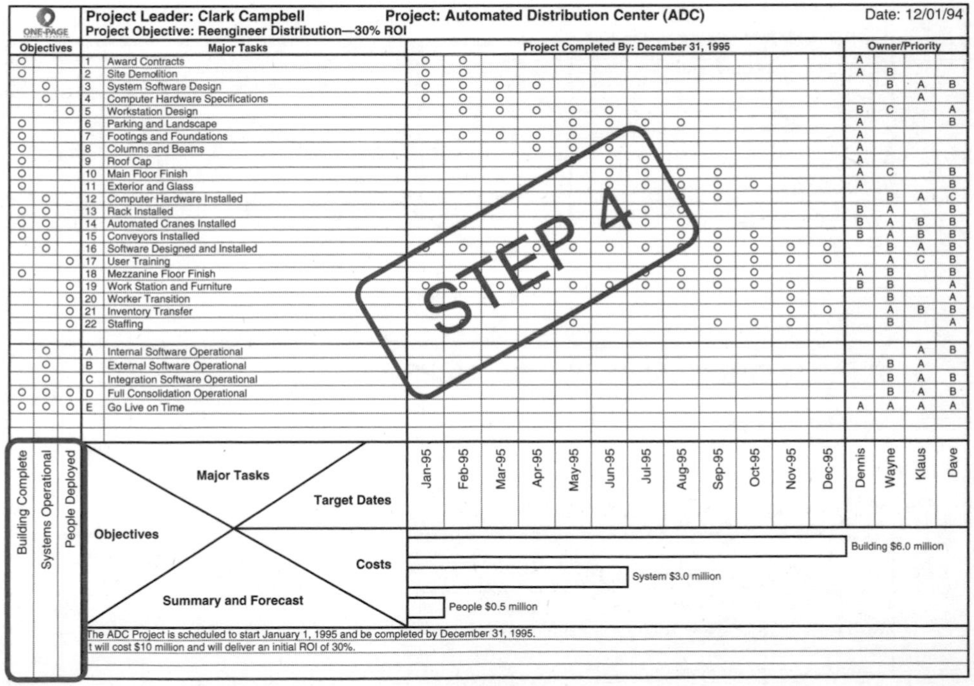

ONE-PAGE

Project Leader: Clark Campbell — Project: Automated Distribution Center (ADC) — Date: 12/01/94

Project Objective: Reengineer Distribution—30% ROI

Project Completed By: December 31, 1995

Building Complete	Systems Operational	People Deployed	#	Major Tasks	Jan-95	Feb-95	Mar-95	Apr-95	May-95	Jun-95	Jul-95	Aug-95	Sep-95	Oct-95	Nov-95	Dec-95	Dennis	Wayne	Klaus	Dave
O			1	Award Contracts	O	O											A			
O			2	Site Demolition	O	O											A	B		
	O		3	System Software Design	O	O	O	O										B	A	B
	O		4	Computer Hardware Specifications	O	O	O												A	
		O	5	Workstation Design		O	O	O	O	O							B	C		A
O			6	Parking and Landscape					O	O	O	O					A			B
O			7	Footings and Foundations		O	O	O	O								A			
O			8	Columns and Beams				O	O	O							A			
O			9	Roof Cap					O	O	O						A			
O			10	Main Floor Finish						O	O	O	O				A	C		B
O			11	Exterior and Glass						O	O	O	O	O			A			B
	O		12	Computer Hardware Installed								O	O					B	A	C
O	O		13	Rack Installed							O	O					B	A		B
O	O		14	Automated Cranes Installed							O	O					B	A	B	B
O	O		15	Conveyors Installed								O	O	O			B	A	B	B
	O		16	Software Designed and Installed	O	O	O	O	O	O	O	O	O	O	O	O		B	A	B
		O	17	User Training									O	O	O	O		A	C	B
O			18	Mezzanine Floor Finish							O	O	O	O			A	B		B
		O	19	Work Station and Furniture	O	O	O	O	O	O	O	O	O	O	O		B	B		A
		O	20	Worker Transition											O			B		A
		O	21	Inventory Transfer											O	O		A	B	B
		O	22	Staffing					O				O	O	O			B		A
	O		A	Internal Software Operational															A	B
	O		B	External Software Operational														B	A	
	O		C	Integration Software Operational														B	A	B
O	O	O	D	Full Consolidation Operational														B	A	B
O	O	O	E	Go Live on Time													A	A	A	A

The ADC Project is scheduled to start January 1, 1995 and be completed by December 31, 1995. It will cost $10 million and will deliver an initial ROI of 30%.

FIGURE 2.6 *The 12 Construction Steps—Step 4*

 To customize this document, download it to your hard drive from the following web site: www.oppmi.com. The document can be opened, edited, and printed using Microsoft Excel or another popular spreadsheet application.

You will want your objectives to be SMART (Simple, Measurable, Attainable, Relevant, and Time based).

Step 5: Major Project Tasks

On the left side of the OPPM, we place the major project tasks (see Figure 2.7). Large projects are really just the sum of many smaller projects that are coordinated and combined to add up to the final project. On the top-most level OPPM, each of these projects is expressed as a task, such as: award contracts to subcontractors, design systems, lay the foundation for a building, and so

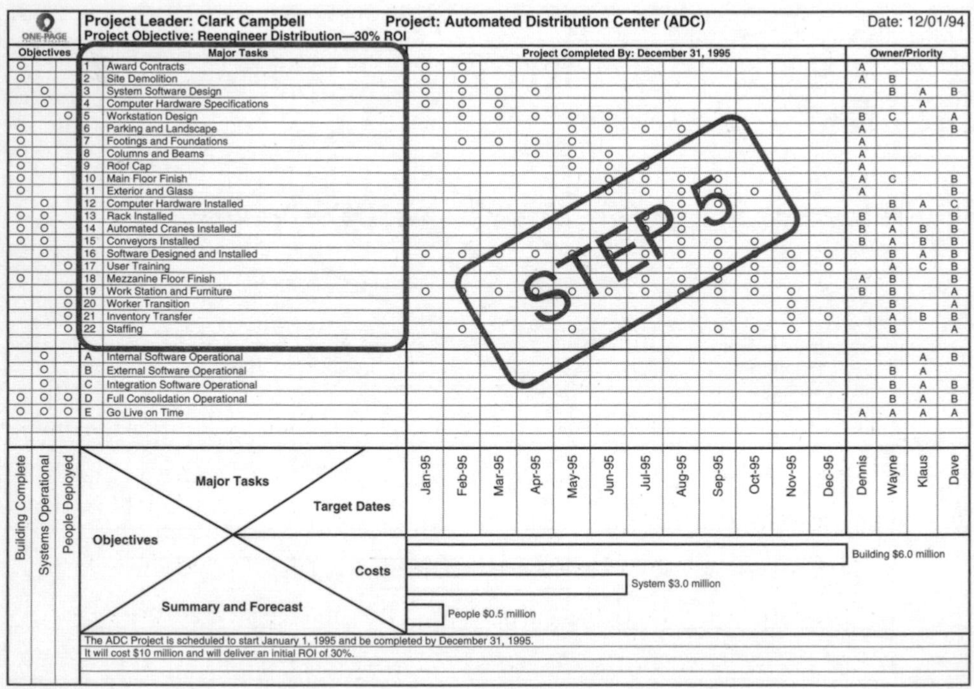

ONE-PAGE

Project Leader: Clark Campbell | Project: Automated Distribution Center (ADC) | Date: 12/01/94

Project Objective: Reengineer Distribution—30% ROI

Building Complete	Systems Operational	People Deployed		Major Tasks	Jan-95	Feb-95	Mar-95	Apr-95	May-95	Jun-95	Jul-95	Aug-95	Sep-95	Oct-95	Nov-95	Dec-95	Dennis	Wayne	Klaus	Dave
O			1	Award Contracts	O	O											A			
O			2	Site Demolition	O	O											A	B		
	O		3	System Software Design	O	O	O	O										B	A	B
	O		4	Computer Hardware Specifications	O	O	O												A	
		O	5	Workstation Design		O	O	O	O	O							B	C		A
O			6	Parking and Landscape					O	O	O	O					A			B
O			7	Footings and Foundations		O	O	O	O								A			
O			8	Columns and Beams				O	O	O							A			
O			9	Roof Cap					O	O	O						A			
O			10	Main Floor Finish						O	O	O	O				A	C		B
O			11	Exterior and Glass						O	O	O	O	O			A			B
	O		12	Computer Hardware Installed								O	O					B	A	C
O	O		13	Rack Installed							O	O					B	A		B
O	O		14	Automated Cranes Installed							O	O					B	A	B	B
O	O		15	Conveyors Installed								O	O	O			B	A	B	B
	O		16	Software Designed and Installed	O	O	O	O	O	O	O	O	O	O	O	O		B	A	B
		O	17	User Training									O	O	O	O		A	C	B
O			18	Mezzanine Floor Finish							O	O	O	O			A	B		B
		O	19	Work Station and Furniture	O	O	O	O	O	O	O	O	O	O	O		B	B		A
		O	20	Worker Transition											O			B		A
		O	21	Inventory Transfer											O	O		A	B	B
		O	22	Staffing		O			O				O	O	O			B		A
	O		A	Internal Software Operational															A	B
	O		B	External Software Operational														B	A	
	O		C	Integration Software Operational														B	A	B
O	O	O	D	Full Consolidation Operational														B	A	B
O	O	O	E	Go Live on Time													A	A	A	A

FIGURE 2.7 *The 12 Construction Steps—Step 5*

 To customize this document, download it to your hard drive from the following web site: www.oppmi.com. The document can be opened, edited, and printed using Microsoft Excel or another popular spreadsheet application.

forth. Tasks should be measurable in terms of their progress so you can gauge their advancement and report on them in the OPPM.

Each task is assigned at least one owner, which is why getting the buy-in from team members for each task is essential. Match tasks with the strengths of the owners whenever possible.

Try to average two to three tasks per reporting period for the length of the project. If a project will run, say, 12 months, 30 or so tasks are about right. Most projects are divided into monthly increments. Some tasks will be as short as one month, whereas others will last the full timeline. Keep in mind that behind each of these tasks you could have another OPPM, or a Microsoft project or Primavera PERT chart.

Step 6: Aligning Tasks with Objectives

In this step, make sure the tasks on your list will, when completed, produce the project's objectives (see Figure 2.8). As you go through your tasks and objectives, it is essential the two match up. All tasks are aligned with at least one objective. Some will naturally connect with more.

This alignment of tasks and objectives often reveals inconsistencies or things missing. The process of alignment is not something done once and left forever. As you work your way through building the OPPM with each step it is natural that you reevaluate succeeding steps and try to constantly improve.

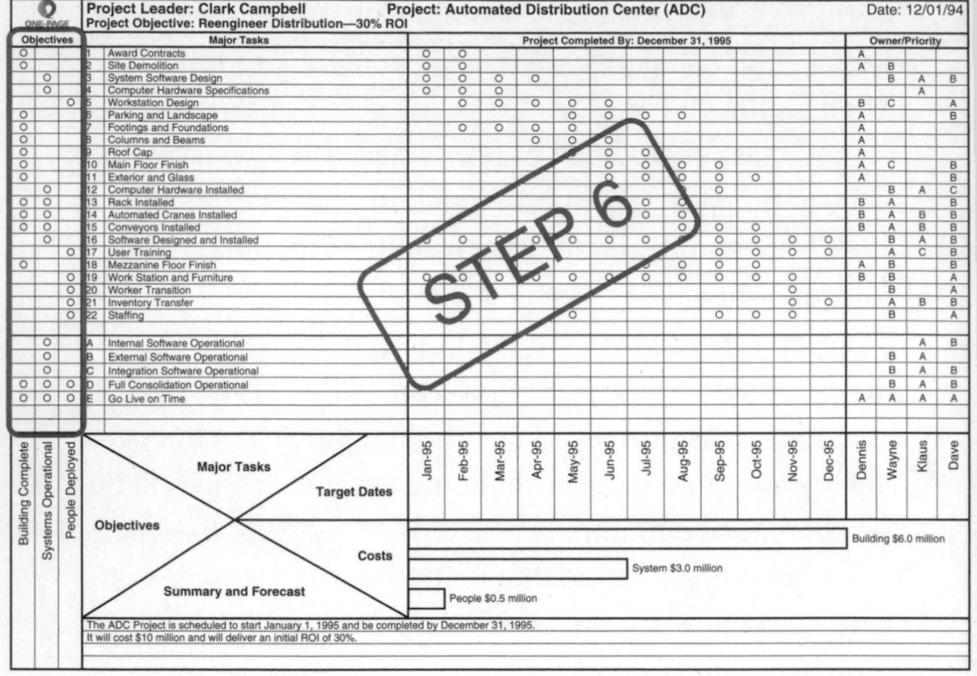

FIGURE 2.8 *The 12 Construction Steps—Step 6*

 To customize this document, download it to your hard drive from the following web site: www.oppmi.com. The document can be opened, edited, and printed using Microsoft Excel or another popular spreadsheet application.

Identifying tasks may reveal a missing objective. You may also find a disproportionate number of tasks aligning with a single objective, therefore suggesting further evaluation of both.

This form of progressive elaboration will enhance the quality of your plan as well as the communicating power of your OPPM.

Step 7: Target Dates

The target dates are found in the rectangle running left to right near the bottom of the OPPM (see Figure 2.9).

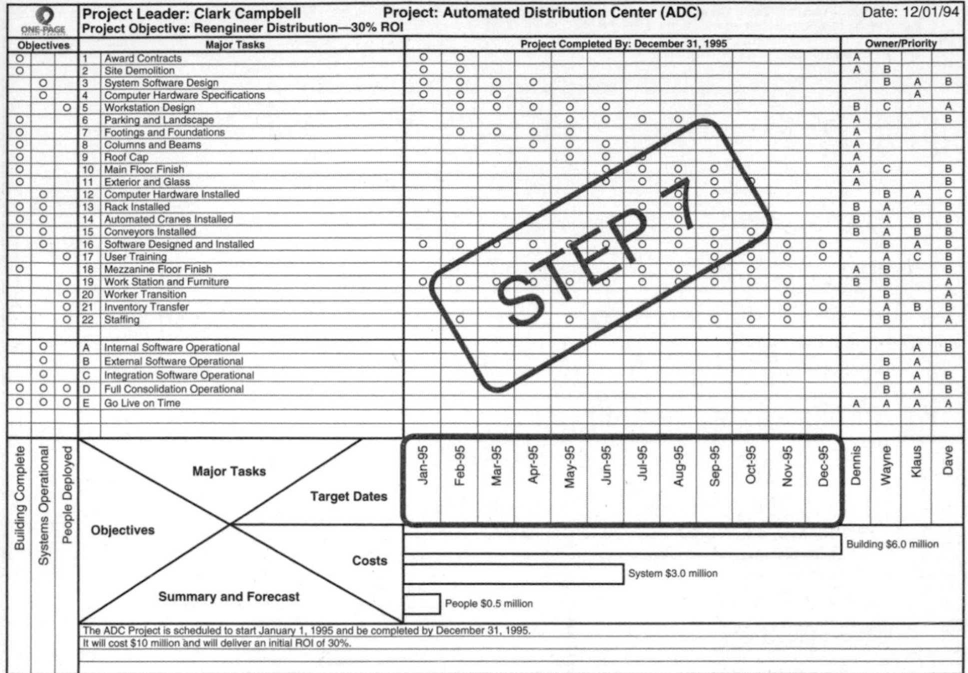

FIGURE 2.9 *The 12 Construction Steps—Step 7*

 To customize this document, download it to your hard drive from the following web site: www.oppmi.com. The document can be opened, edited, and printed using Microsoft Excel or another popular spreadsheet application.

Here we break down the timeline into discrete steps, most commonly monthly (though a short project may have weekly or bi-weekly steps, and a very long project may have commensurately longer periods). Every period does not need to be the same length. Keep in mind that when you let everyone know the project's timeline and time increments, you magnify your responsibility for meeting them. As with tasks, you need buy-in for time commitments from all concerned.

Step 8: Aligning Tasks to the Timeline

This step involves creating a timeline for each of the project's tasks (see Figure 2.10). We place an empty circle in the boxes alongside the task, representing the start, length, and completion date for each task. If the task will take seven months and the time buckets are in monthly increments, then there will be seven circles next to this task. As each task is completed, the aligned circle will be filled in.

Each team members will approach the task timeline discovery process with very different kinds of thinking.

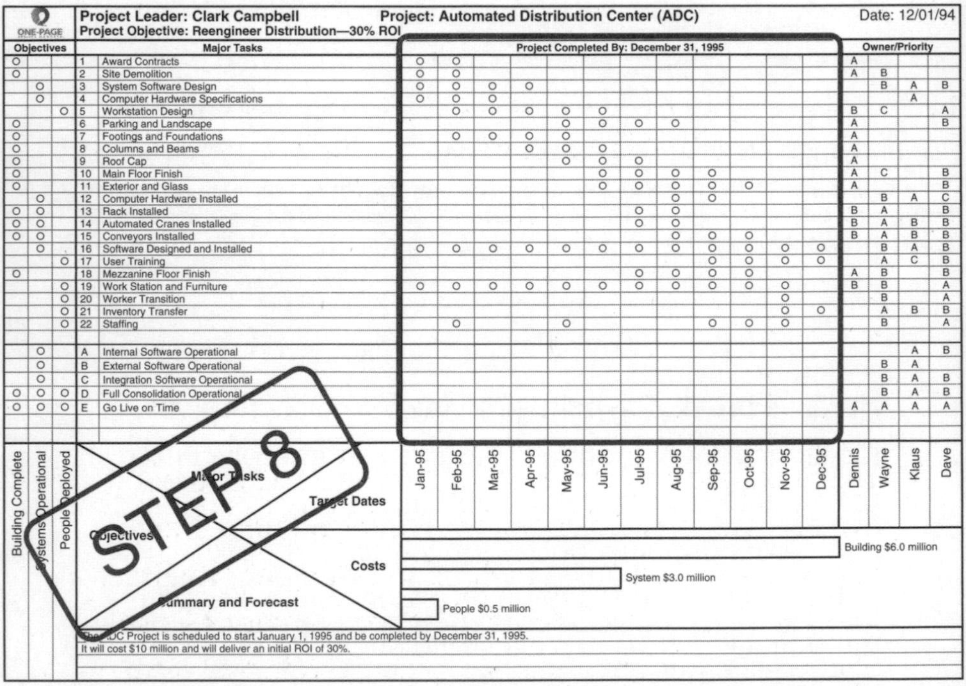

ONE-PAGE
Project Leader: Clark Campbell — Project: Automated Distribution Center (ADC) — Date: 12/01/94
Project Objective: Reengineer Distribution—30% ROI

Building Complete	Systems Operational	People Deployed	#	Major Tasks	Jan-95	Feb-95	Mar-95	Apr-95	May-95	Jun-95	Jul-95	Aug-95	Sep-95	Oct-95	Nov-95	Dec-95	Dennis	Wayne	Klaus	Dave
Objectives				Major Tasks	Project Completed By: December 31, 1995												Owner/Priority			
O			1	Award Contracts	O	O											A			
O			2	Site Demolition	O	O											A	B		
	O		3	System Software Design	O	O	O	O										B	A	B
	O		4	Computer Hardware Specifications	O	O	O												A	
		O	5	Workstation Design		O	O	O	O	O							B	C		A
O			6	Parking and Landscape					O	O	O	O					A			B
O			7	Footings and Foundations		O	O	O	O								A			
O			8	Columns and Beams				O	O	O							A			
O			9	Roof Cap					O	O	O						A			
O			10	Main Floor Finish						O	O	O	O				A	C		B
O			11	Exterior and Glass						O	O	O	O	O			A			B
	O		12	Computer Hardware Installed								O	O					B	A	C
O	O		13	Rack Installed							O	O					B	A		B
O	O		14	Automated Cranes Installed							O	O					B	A	B	B
O	O		15	Conveyors Installed								O	O	O			B	A	B	B
	O		16	Software Designed and Installed	O	O	O	O	O	O	O	O	O	O	O	O		B	A	B
		O	17	User Training									O	O	O	O		A	C	B
O			18	Mezzanine Floor Finish							O	O	O	O			A	B		B
		O	19	Work Station and Furniture	O	O	O	O	O	O	O	O	O	O	O		B	B		A
		O	20	Worker Transition											O			B		A
		O	21	Inventory Transfer											O	O		A	B	B
		O	22	Staffing		O			O				O	O	O			B		A
	O		A	Internal Software Operational															A	B
	O		B	External Software Operational														B	A	
	O		C	Integration Software Operational														B	A	B
O	O	O	D	Full Consolidation Operational														B	A	B
O	O	O	E	Go Live on Time													A	A	A	A

STEP 8

Major Tasks — Target Dates — Objectives — Costs — Summary and Forecast

Costs: Building $6.0 million; System $3.0 million; People $0.5 million

The ADC Project is scheduled to start January 1, 1995 and be completed by December 31, 1995.
It will cost $10 million and will deliver an initial ROI of 30%.

FIGURE 2.10 *The 12 Construction Steps—Step 8*

 To customize this document, download it to your hard drive from the following web site: www.oppmi.com. The document can be opened, edited, and printed using Microsoft Excel or another popular spreadsheet application.

Some start at the beginning and think forward. Some start with the end in mind and ponder backward. Your most creative often think "out of the box" in a random way. It is critical that you encourage each approach in order to facilitate the creation of a robust plan.

Step 9: Aligning Tasks to Owners

Tasks have owners, usually one, rarely more than three. No matter how many owners per task, a priority between owners must be set. There is almost always *one* main owner per task. The letter A on the OPPM designates that owner as the primary one (see Figure 2.11). A subowner would be designated as a B owner, and someone subordinate to that owner would be a C owner. Who owns what is decided through a process of negotiation between team members, with you as project manager providing leadership and, if need be, mediation.

Step 10: Subjective Tasks

This is the portion of the OPPM that deals with subjective or qualitative tasks. Not everything about a project can be quantified on a timeline: software performance, for example, cannot. A computer programmer's sense of adequate performance may be quite different from an end user's. Think of cell phone service. A dropped call is considered unacceptable, but what about sporadic static? Is that acceptable once in a while?

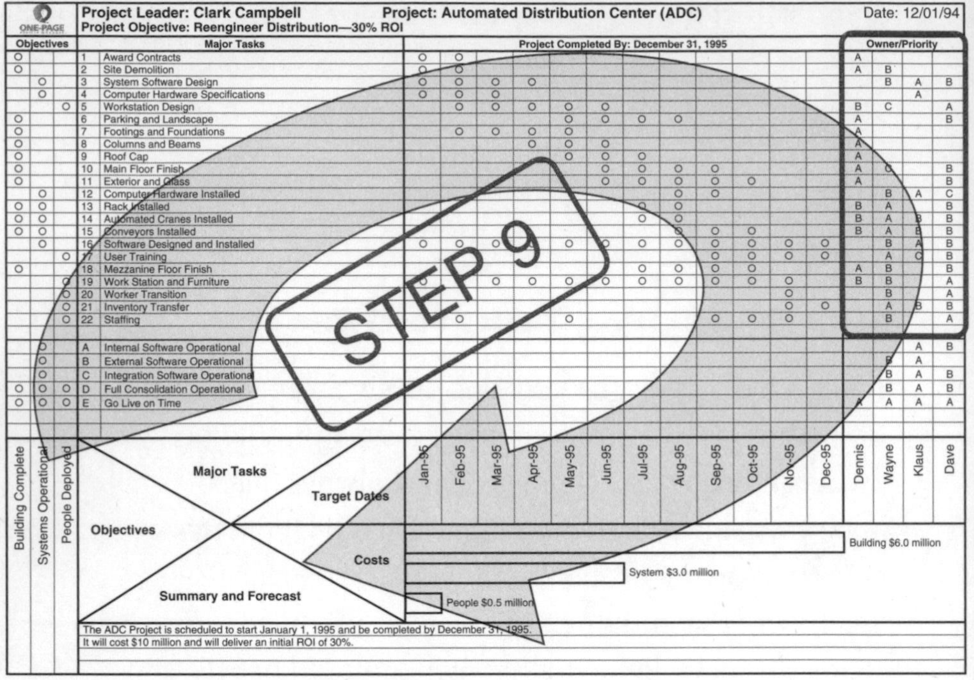

FIGURE 2.11 *The 12 Construction Steps—Step 9*

 To customize this document, download it to your hard drive from the following web site: www.oppmi.com. The document can be opened, edited, and printed using Microsoft Excel or another popular spreadsheet application.

Situations like these are subjective. This section is where one places the subjective aspects of a project (see Figure 2.12). Be sure, though, that the objectives and owners are aligned with these subjective tasks just as they are with the more quantifiable tasks. Judgments concerning performance against these tasks will be shown as red, yellow, or green.

Step 11: Costs

The lower right-hand side of the OPPM is where the budget is represented (see Figure 2.13). The budget is dealt

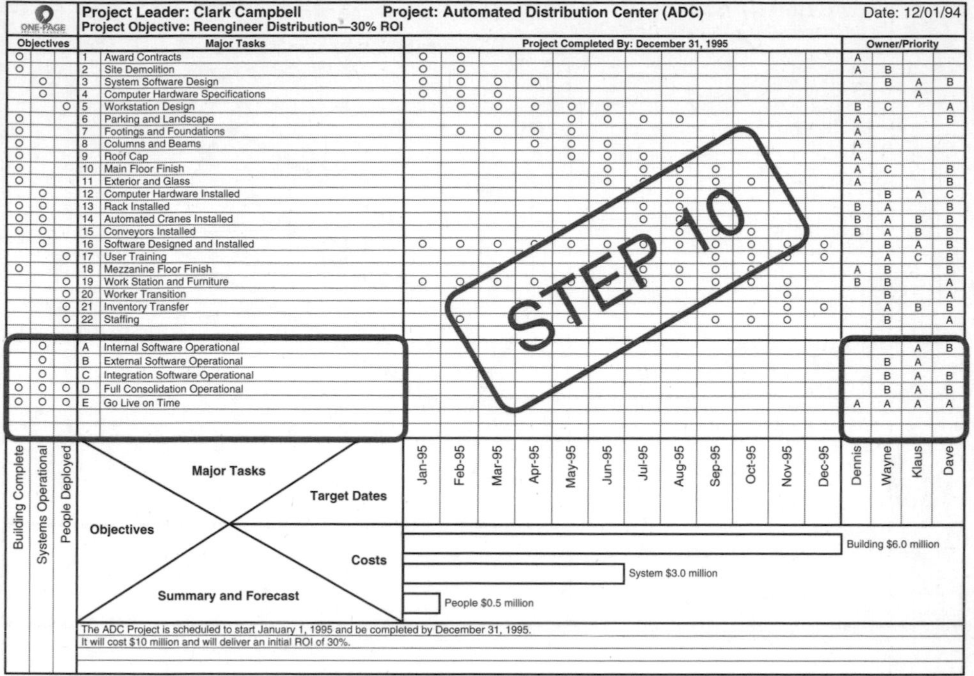

FIGURE 2.12 *The 12 Construction Steps—Step 10*

with simply, using a bar graph for each portion of the budget. When the portion is on budget, it is depicted with green. When it is running over budget but is recoverable, it is shown in yellow. And when it is incurably over budget, it is depicted with red.

Showing the budget on the OPPM is easy; deriving it is much more difficult. Before you draw up the budget, know all your costs. Include provisions for incremental increases, such as those due to uncertainty or potential changes in the project.

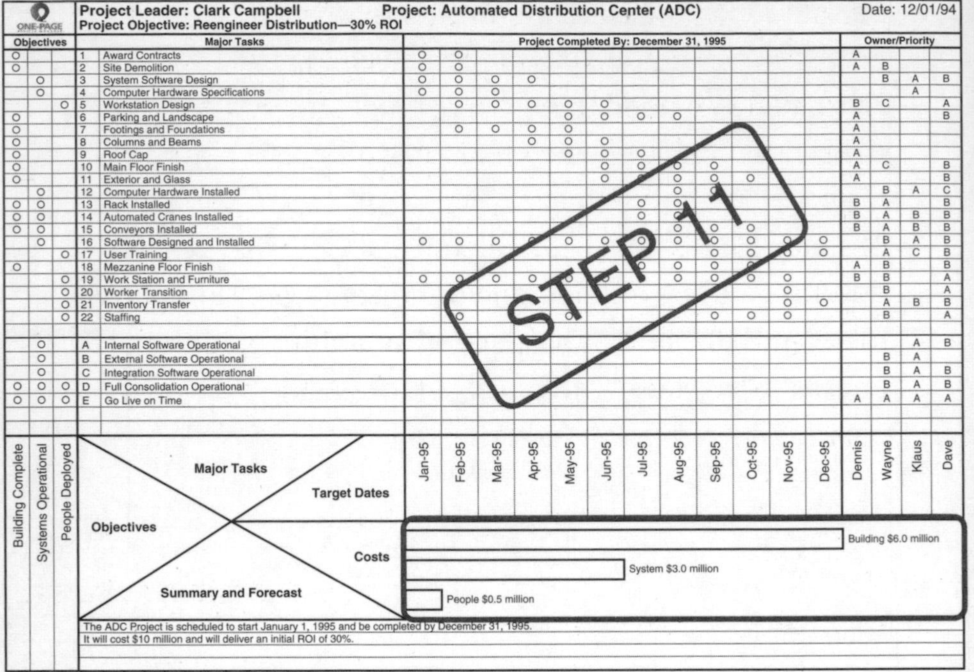

FIGURE 2.13 *The 12 Construction Steps—Step 11*

Also, this is the area where you can plan and track a few of the project's essential metrics other than money.

Step 12: Summary and Forecast

A good summary clears up any ambiguities or glaring questions and heads off potential future misunderstandings. Everybody should now be "reading from the same page"—both literally and metaphorically.

The summary is used to answer questions prompted by the graphics, not to explain the graphics themselves.

Your language should add further expectation to your analysis—a what next to the why (see Figure 2.14). Here, you will need to be as succinct and comprehensive as possible. The OPPM has a limited amount of space for the summary. This is by design. The lack of space forces you to be selective about what you describe and be efficient in your discussion. Do not try to expand the summary space by attaching additional pages or diagrams. The power of the OPPM rests, in part, on the fact it is, well, one page.

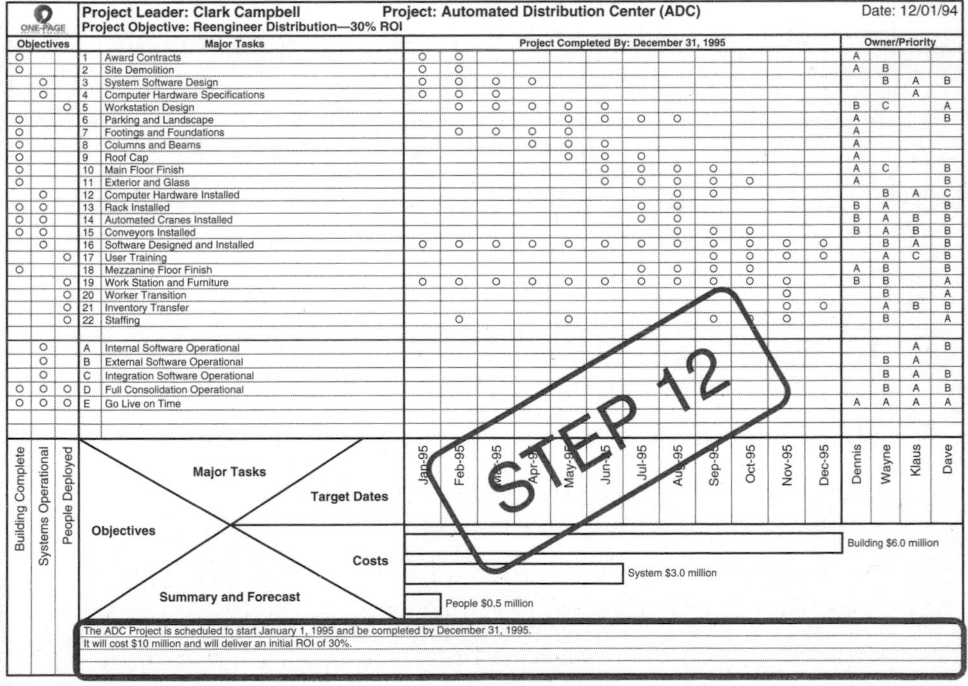

FIGURE 2.14 *The 12 Construction Steps—Step 12*

 To customize this document, download it to your hard drive from the following web site: www.oppmi.com. The document can be opened, edited, and printed using Microsoft Excel or another popular spreadsheet application.

FIVE STEPS TO CREATING A REPORT USING THE OPPM

Creating an OPPM report for each time period (usually monthly) involves five steps. You meet with your project's owners near the conclusion of each Target Date and complete the following tasks:

1. ***Bold the Target Date.***
2. ***Fill in Major Task progress.*** This is where you fill in the dots. While filling in the dots is easy, getting agreement from team members on which to fill in or not fill in is often anything but easy. Your job as project manager is to bring the team together and communicate unambiguously.
3. ***Designate qualitative performance.*** This involves using colors. We define green as adequate performance, yellow as worrisome performance, and red as dangerous performance. As with filling in the dots, agreeing to the colors can be a source of tension and require negotiation.
4. ***Report expenditures.*** Figures should come from the accounting department, which has to be in agreement with how the budget is portrayed on the OPPM.
5. ***Write the summary and forecast*** (see Figure 2.15).

You now have the basics of creating and using the OPPM.

In Jeffrey K. Liker's book, *The Toyota Way,* he asserts:

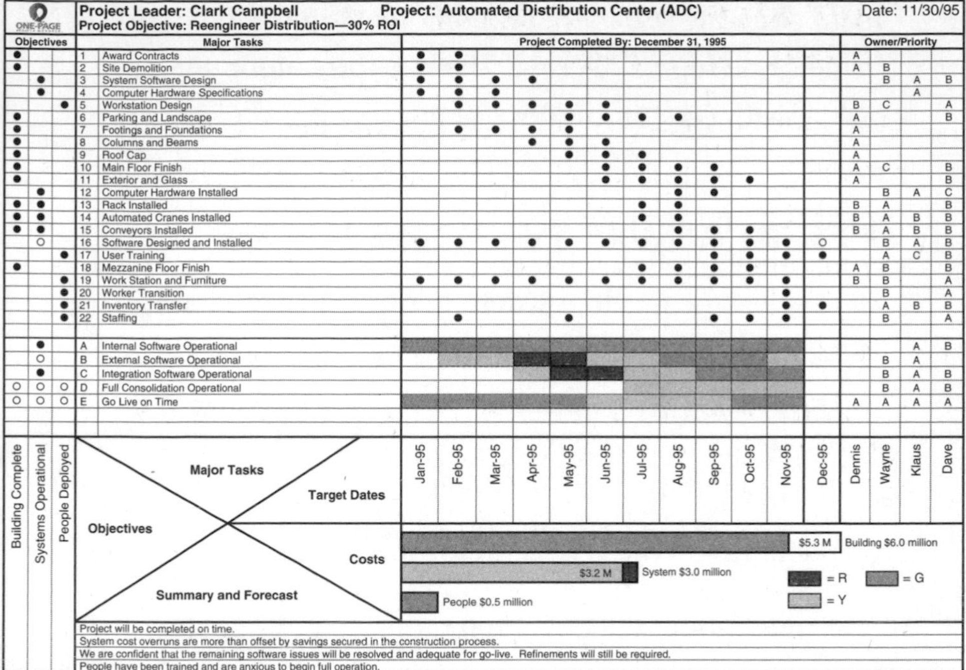

FIGURE 2.15 *The November ADC Report*

 To customize this document, download it to your hard drive from the following web site: www.oppmi.com. The document can be opened, edited, and printed using Microsoft Excel or another popular spreadsheet application.

> *the most time-consuming and difficult way to understand complex ideas is to have to decipher a lengthy report . . . More efficient is the visual approach. Acting on the fact that people are visually oriented, new employees at Toyota learn to communicate with as few words as possible and with visual aids. The A3 report is a key part of this process. [p. 244.]*

This book is about combining the OPPM with the A3. As an executive who oversees projects, you need to provide executive direction, and that includes having your team generate sufficient and efficient communication using these reports. We will discuss the combination of OPPM with A3s in Chapters 4 and 5.

TIPS TO ASSURE THE OPPM IS USED

Here are some tips that will help ensure the OPPM is used effectively throughout your organization:

- Be sure your project managers and team members understand the value of the tool. You can try to force your people to use the OPPM by making its use mandatory, but making team members willing believers is much more effective than coercion. When they understand how simple it is to use and how powerful and valuable it can be, they will naturally want to use it. But they first have to understand the tool's value. You may want to encourage them to read this book and then review the free downloadable forms available at www.oppmi.com. Having even one person in your organization become competent, confident, and conversant in the OPPM should be enough to get your entire organization behind it. That one person becomes the messenger, the advocate, the champion throughout your organization. Our experience has shown that once a project manager begins to use the OPPM, acceptance, enthusiasm, and even expectations follow.
- Make clear that you and other upper-level managers will not read long reports or insufficient summaries

of projects but will read OPPMs. This will encourage those working on projects to make the OPPM part of their communications toolkit as quickly as possible.

- Have a standard version of the OPPM in your organization. Do not allow numerous versions to be developed as this will make the tool cumbersome and ineffective. Of course, different types of projects will require the OPPM to be tweaked to meet their needs. However, you should have one standard version of the OPPM and allow only relatively minor modifications to it to meet the needs of individual projects. We suggest as a template the one available on www.oppmi.com, as shown in Figure 2.2. You want to keep things simple, so limit the variations of the OPPM used within your organization.
- Be sure the OPPM is used universally within your organization. If upper managers like you are not committed to its use, it will never be adapted and effectively used.

You benefit from the use of the OPPM because it:

- Dramatically reduces the time it will take you to review a project.
- Causes your project managers to improve the quality, timing, and cost-effectiveness of their projects by making them review all the important parts of a project on a regular basis and by making the lines of responsibility clear.

- Makes clear to you certain salient pieces of information that traditional project summaries often obscure, such as who the owners of specific parts of a project are and where all the important parts of a project stand in terms of meeting their deadlines and budget.
- Reduces the time, people, and resources needed to convey important information about projects to upper management, giving project teams more time to spend doing what they really want to do—namely, work on their projects.
- Uses graphics that visually display performance against scope, time, and costs.
- Will reduce and, in some instances, eliminate the need for formal project review meetings.
- Prompts the right questions.
- Depicts yesterday's vision, today's performance, and tomorrow's forecast.

HOW TO READ THE OPPM

The OPPM has several essential parts that are easily understood. In fact, you could probably look at the OPPM without any instruction and figure out most of its workings; it is that intuitive. But the brief descriptions that follow will help you understand some of the thinking behind each part. Refer to Figures 2.2 and 2.15 to show how the part fits in with the overall OPPM.

1. *The Header:* This is very basic and includes the project's name, the project's leader, the project's objective, and the date of the report. At a glance, you see what the project is about, who is in charge, what the project is trying to accomplish. You complete this together with your project manager.

2. *The Owners:* This part tells you who is in charge (who owns) each part of the project. Responsibility is made public here. An "A" owner is the primary owner of that task, the one who is most responsible for seeing it through to completion.

3. *The Matrix:* This is the heart of the OPPM. It is where various parts of the OPPM come together. Use it as a compass to point you to the pieces of information (objectives, major tasks, deadlines, budget, summary, and forecast) you are interested in at that particular moment.

4. *Project Objectives:* These might also be called subobjectives because they are subordinate to the project's overall objective. Some suggestions here by you to your project manager might prove helpful in further clarifying your expectations simply shown in the header. This is also a good place to reinforce the SMART model for writing objectives as previously discussed.

5. *Major Project Tasks:* This is arguably the most important component of the OPPM. Here you see the major tasks that need to be finished in order for the project to be completed. The numbered tasks are objective tasks, which are tasks that can be objectively measured. Subjective tasks, which are lettered, are tasks not lending themselves to objective measurement; they are qualitative rather than quantitative. Many OPPM users have found that the qualitative area is a good place to show Earned Value (see Appendix C) or to track for that project the most important component of the triple constraint.

6. *Aligning Tasks with Objectives:* Here is an interpretative aspect of the OPPM. You look at the tasks and objectives with an eye to making sure the tasks listed will, when completed, produce the objectives you are aiming for. The circles tell you which objective (or objectives) is tied to which tasks. Part of the power of the OPPM is that it will show you how different parts of a project relate. In this case, we are using the tool to see how tasks and objectives work together. You really need to do this analysis only at the beginning of the project.

Once you are sure the tasks will lead to your objective, you will not need to visit this again, unless you change the project's objectives (which is actually fairly common). As a project progresses, you and your project team may reevaluate succeeding steps, similar in concept of Kaizen, or continuous improvement. Some tasks may be aligned with two objectives, which is acceptable, but most tasks are aligned with just one objective, and all tasks must be aligned with at least one objective. If a task does not contribute to meeting one of the objectives, it should not be there.

You are looking for both content and balance here. For example, a project team with deep experience in one subobjective area will overload tasks aligned to their expertise, where tasks necessary to other, less-experienced subobjectives may receive insufficient delineation.

7. *Target Dates:* This is where you can easily see how well each task is proceeding in terms of its time progression and deadline. The vertical line tells you where on the timeline you are now. The timeline is usually divided into months. However, the time units do not have to be months. Short projects may be divided into weekly increments, whereas long ones may be divided into bi-monthly or quarterly increments. Also, some projects may have different length buckets on a single timeline. The dots (used with the objective tasks) indicate the months allotted for each task. When a dot is filled in, it is complete. If a task has dots not filled in and the vertical line is to the right of the dots, it indicates the task is behind schedule.

We use color and a bar graph to depict subjective tasks. If a task is green, then performance is adequate, whereas yellow indicates performance is worrisome but solvable. Red indicates performance issues are seriously endangering cost, scope, or timing.

8. *Costs:* This is done as a bar graph representing the budget. The budget stands alone and is not graphically aligned to the timeline. This graph provides a quick, easy-to-understand picture of where the budget is at any given moment.

9. *Summary and Forecast:* This small section of the OPPM is small for a reason—to make sure there are no lengthy explanations. It is where the project manager and project team address issues raised in the body of the report. It is not a place to restate the obvious, but it is a place to answer the questions posed by the graphics and communicate remedies and expectations for the near-term future.

A LITTLE MORE . . .

These are the basic parts of the OPPM. Let me make a few more comments about how to read and use this tool.

- ***Pay attention to the colors.*** Greens you expect, yellows are cause for concern, and reds really need your attention.
- ***Pay attention to the dots.*** Open circles to the left of the heavy vertical date line are cause for concern. The more empty dots to the left of a line associated with a given task, the more behind schedule that task is. And the more behind schedule a task is, the more that task needs your attention.
- ***Look at the budget line and make sure the project is running at or near budget.*** If not, give the budget your attention. Find out from the project manager and the owners what the problems are. Yellows may be adequately addressed in the Summary and Forecast section. Reds prompt a face-to-face meeting in most organizations.
- ***Pay attention to owners.*** It is obvious that when an owner has several tasks in trouble, that owner has some explaining to do. Hold him or her accountable. But don't ignore the positive. An owner who, during

a project, consistently finishes tasks on or before schedule or on or under budget should be recognized. The OPPM helps hold people accountable, and when someone is performing well, they deserve positive recognition, as does that person's team. There is power in appreciation. "When recognition is applied to good management, it serves as an accelerator of employee performance and engagement." (*The Carrot Principle*, by Adrian Gostick and Chester Elton.) In her book, *The Power of Acknowledgement*, Judith Umlas writes, "Recognizing good work leads to high energy, great feelings, high-quality performance and terrific results." Our experience has shown that leaders who 1. Enlarge the audience; 2. Embed a cadence; and 3. Amplify receptivity actually magnify the power of their appreciation efforts. OPPMs substantially assist in communicating exceptional project performance to a larger *audience* with an anticipated *cadence*. They combine reliable data in a standard methodology therefore insuring eager *receptivity* for the acknowledgement of great work.

- ***Read the summary and forecast.*** It is where you will learn the whys behind the information presented in the OPPM and the future view at the time the OPPM was issued.

Understand that the OPPM does not provide you with a great deal of detail. You can't see or understand the nitty-gritty going's on of a project by reading the OPPM. The challenge that a particular task has meeting its deadline is usually not obvious on the OPPM (unless discussed in the summary and forecast). This absence of detail is intentional. The OPPM is an effective communication tool for upper management precisely because it lacks great detail. You don't usually need to know all the details. What the OPPM gives you is the big picture, the broad strokes. That's the power and the beauty of the tool. If there is an aspect to a project you want to know more about, you can always ask the project manager or the project's owners. The OPPM highlights what is important to upper management, and it leaves out the rest.

CHAPTER 3

OPPM for ISO 9000

O.C. Tanner had the most advanced quality management systems in our industry. I'm not just saying that; we had statistics that backed up this claim. No question, we were the quality leader. But our competition had something we did not have, namely an ISO 9001:2000 certification. Even though our quality metrics exceeded our competitors', lacking this certification put us at a competitive disadvantage. We decided it would be practical and valuable to secure an ISO 9001:2000 certification. Internally, we called the project ISO 9000—a kind of generic name for the type of certification we were seeking. ISO 9001:2000 is part of the family of the ISO 9000 certifications.

Again, OPPMs may be used alone or together as part of an A3 report. This chapter addresses the OPPM specifically. You will see this same OPPM combined with its A3 in Chapter 5.

ISO CERTIFICATION: WHAT IT IS

For those unfamiliar with ISO certifications, let us briefly explain them. The organization that oversees ISO certifications is the International Organization for Standardization, founded in 1947 and based in Geneva, Switzerland. ISO seeks to establish standards within industries that are benchmarks by which organizations can measure themselves. Typically, these standards are technically oriented.

There are various ISO standards. The two best known are ISO 9000 and ISO 14000, with the former addressing quality issues and the latter addressing environmental standards.

The ISO 9001:2000 certification includes procedures that cover a business's key processes and ways of monitoring and keeping track of these processes. It also includes standards for identifying product defects and strategies for eliminating such defects. According to ISO:

> *"ISO 9000 is concerned with 'quality management.' This means what the organization does to enhance customer satisfaction by meeting customer and applicable regulatory requirements and continually to improve its performance in this regard."*

About the ISO 9001:2000 standard, which was established in the year 2000 and is now widely implemented, the ISO says, "ISO 9001:2000 is used if you are seeking to establish a management system that provides confidence in the conformance of your product to established or specified requirements." It includes, according to the ISO, five sections:

1. Activities used to supply your products
2. Quality management systems
3. Management responsibility
4. Resource management and measurement
5. Analysis and improvement

EARNING THE ISO CERTIFICATION

Obtaining certification is a complex, labor-intensive, time-consuming process. Each of our processes needed explicit quality objectives and documentation. In a general sense, we had to map out key processes and monitor and measure them all with an eye toward ensuring we were maintaining the desired level of quality. Even the quality of suppliers was addressed. And, as a company, we needed to determine the skills required for each and every job in our company, train each employee, and measure how effective that training was. Documenting procedures and results is a major part of ISO certification.

Getting certified is not easy or cheap. We already had implemented a number of programs based on the work of such management gurus as Joseph M. Juran, W. Edwards Deming, Philip Crosby, and Shigeo Shingo, as well as Lean Manufacturing. But as I noted earlier, we needed to obtain this certification in order to communicate to the market our commitment to quality and our dedication to continuous quality improvement.

Marketing may have been the initial impetus, but an amplified culture of quality resulted from imbedding ISO disciplines. On a more personal note, the quality orientation of ISO certification matched perfectly the philosophy of our company's founder, Obert C. Tanner, who died in 1993 after guiding the O.C. Tanner Company for 64 years. On a brass plaque in our headquarters, we have a quote from Obert: "We seek to touch the fringes of perfection." This became the slogan of our ISO project. ISO certification served to further improve our quality, and it helped us touch the fringes of perfection.

Let's look now at the OPPM we created to manage this ISO project.

APPLYING THE OPPM

The ISO 9000 project did not require much customization of the standard OPPM (Figure 3.1). The standard elements included the objectives, which are listed in the bottom left corner of the form. Note that the first objective is Organizational Commitment. This refers to the commitment of the organization toward obtaining the ISO certification. Of course, all projects require a strong commitment from the organization. But with a project like ISO certification, the absolute commitment of everyone in the organization, including management, is absolutely essential, which is why we made it one of our

ONE-PAGE

Project Leader: Larry Hamilton **Project: ISO 9000** Date: Sept 30

Project Objective: Achieve ISO 9001:2000 Certificaton

Organizational Commitment	Develop Quality Manual	Develop Procedures	Develop Work Instructions	Develop Records	Develop Internal Audit System	#	Major Tasks	April	May	June	July	August	September	October	November	December	January	February	Executive Management	Project Manager	ISO Project Teams	Internal Auditors	ISO Consultant
							Definition Phase																
●						1	Establish Development Team	●	●										A	B			
●						2	Train Development Team	●	●											A	B		B
●						3	Develop Process Map	●	●											B			A
●						4	Select Registrar	●	●	●									B	A			
	●	●	●			5	Define Level II Procedures	●	●	●	●									A	B		B
	●	●	●			6	Quality Manual	●	●	●	●								B	B	B		A
			●	●		7	Work Instructions and Forms	●	●	●	●										A		B
		●	●	●	●	8	Records	●	●	●	●										A		
							Implementation Phase																
		●	●	●	●	9	Train New Processes			●	●	●								B	A		B
		●				10	Publish Quality Manual				●	●								A			B
				●		11	New Forms/Work Instructions			●	●										A		B
		●	●			12	Put Procedures under Document Control			●	●									A	B		B
			●			13	Implement Procedures			●	●	●							A	B	B		B
	○	○	○	○	○	14	Awareness Training			●	●	○							B	A			
							Verification Phase																
	●					15	Develop and Train Internal Auditors				●	●										B	A
●	●					16	Implement Internal Auditing Program				●	●							B	B		A	B
	●	●	●	●	●	17	Conduct Management Review				●	●							A	B		B	
	●	●	●	●	●	18	Conduct Pre-Audit Assessment					●	●							B		A	
			○			19	Pre-Audit Corrective Actions						○	○					B	A	B		
							Validation Phase																
○	○	○	○	○	○	20	Registration Audit							●	○					A			B
○		○	○	○	○	21	Corrective Actions							○	○	○			B		A		
○						22	Certification									○	○		A	A	A	A	A
○						23	Project Closeout										○	○		A	B	B	B
●						A	Organizational Commitment												A	B	B	B	B
○	○	○	○	○	○	B	Our Performance												B	A	B	B	B
○	○	○	○	○	○	C	Consultant Performance												B	B	B	B	A
							# Procedures Completed:	1/17	6/17	12/17	17/20	17/19	19/19										

Objectives | Major Tasks | Target Dates | Costs and Metrics | Summary and Forecast

Project Completed By: Feb

Owner/Priority

	Completed / Expended	Required / Budgeted
Expenses	135	150
Work Instructions	580	580
Records	307	307

■ Expended □ Budgeted ■ Completed □ Required ■ = G ■ = Y

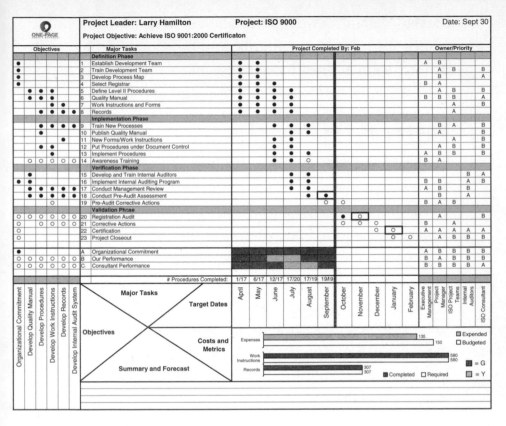

FIGURE 3.1 *The September ISO 9000 Report*

 To customize this document, download it to your hard drive from the following web site: www.oppmi.com. The document can be opened, edited, and printed using Microsoft Excel or another popular spreadsheet application.

objectives. Without such commitment, it is easy for other seemingly more pressing business issues to take priority. ISO certification is easy to place on the back burner, and when that happens, it is unlikely the organization will ever get the certification it wants. We also listed organizational commitment under Major Tasks (Task A).

As mentioned, written materials and processes are a very important part of the ISO certification process. The remaining objectives, including Develop

Quality Manual, Develop Procedures, Develop Work Instructions, Develop Records, and Develop Internal Audit System address these needs.

Phases of the Project

We broke the project down into four phases, which is somewhat unusual. We delineated the phases on the OPPM with horizontal gray lines, each labeled with a phase: Definition Phase, Implementation Phase, Verification Phase, and Validation Phase. These phases represent an often-used standard methodology for ISO implementation projects, helping the project team break the project down into manageable chunks it can more easily focus on. These phases are comprised of 23 quantitative tasks (1 through 23) and three qualitative tasks (A through C).

As an indication of the complexity of this project, most of these tasks had their own OPPM, such as Task 6, Quality Manual. Creating this manual was a significant project by itself. Some tasks, such as Task 14, Awareness Training, did not require a full OPPM. Here, the trainer had on her desk a simple task list that consisted of who was to be trained and when. But many of the other tasks were sufficiently large and complex that they needed to be broken down more granularly into additional owners, objectives, and timelines.

One strength of the OPPM is that it can be used to drill down further and further when necessary, making even the most complex project suitable for the OPPM.

On the qualitative side, Tasks A (Organizational Commitment), B (Our Performance) and C (Consultant Performance) were so critical that we wanted to track each of these with a color line throughout the project. With projects in which you engage the services of a consultant, it is very helpful to have a place on the OPPM where the consultant gives you a score and you give the consultant a score. That's what we've done here with Task B (Our Performance) and Task C (Consultant Performance). It is a powerful incentive to keep our consultant and us on task by having our performance and the consultant's on public display via the OPPM. Chapter 7 of *The One-Page Project Manager for IT Projects* provides detailed explanation and examples of how to use OPPMs to manage consultants and their projects.

On the right-hand side of the form, we have the Owner/Priority section. We broke the owners into five groups: Executive Management, Project Manager, ISO Project Teams, Internal Auditors, and ISO Consultant. We've said elsewhere that we don't usually have an owner outside the company. In this situation, we made an exception by making the consultant an owner for four of the major tasks. We did this because the consultant played a very important role relating to certain tasks; it made sense to designate him as an owner. For example, Task 3, Develop Process Map, has the consultant as the top priority owner. That's because we did not know how to do this task and the consultant did, and, therefore, the primary responsibility for completing this task fell to the consultant. There are no absolutes in the use of the OPPM. It is highly flexible. The project is the important thing. The OPPM is for the project; the project is not for the OPPM.

The timeline (the horizontal line near the bottom labeled Target Dates) shows the length of the project (11 months) and the frequency of the reporting periods (monthly). Choosing monthly time buckets for the reporting period was arbitrary. We could have divided the time into bi-weekly periods, for example, but we felt that monthly reporting was sufficiently frequent to keep the project on track and not so frequent as to make the reporting too time-consuming. Progress on the ISO 9000 project was reported monthly to the full management staff using the OPPM as the principal PowerPoint slide.

A critical, absolutely essential element of ISO 9000 is the identification and documentation of procedures. The number of these procedures is determined as you go through the project, and it can change over time. The procedures have to be thoroughly documented and accompanied with work instructions and records. We tracked this documentation on the OPPM in two ways. One was under the various tasks.

The second way is unique to this OPPM. You see it on the line directly above the Target Dates section labeled # Procedures Completed. In April, we thought we needed 17 procedures, and one had been thoroughly documented and completed (which is why the April box has 1/17 in it). By July, we had documented 17 procedures but reasoned we needed three more (17/20), which means we had added three procedures to the

17 we had originally. But by September, we figured we needed only 19 procedures and that all had been completed (19/19).

Also, as mentioned previously, we use bold squares to highlight major milestones. This OPPM has three such squares. The first was Task 18, Conduct Pre-Audit Assessment. It was to be completed in September, which is noted in the bold square indicating this date. This task, as shown on the form, was completed on time. The second milestone was Task 20, Registration Audit, which was to be completed by November. And the third was Task 22, Certification, which was to be completed by January. These were the three most critical tasks in the project.

Another variation of the standard OPPM found with this form is the cost section, which has been expanded to read Costs and Metrics. The first bar, Expenses, shows we spent $105,000 out of a budgeted $150,000. It is yellow because we were a little over budget.

You will see that this section also includes Work Instructions and Records. These are the supporting building blocks and metrics needed for the procedures. There were 19 procedures in our company, under which there were 580 work instructions. There can be one procedure that requires 100 work instructions, for instance, while another procedure requires only one or two. The records document the processes. One value of the OPPM with a project as complex as ISO 9000 is that anyone with this tool can assess the progress of the project with one look.

Speaking of how well the OPPM relates the progress of the project, note that at the time of this OPPM, two tasks were behind schedule and one ahead of schedule. Task 14, Awareness Training, should have been completed in August, but we are now in September, and it has yet to be completed. Task 19, the Pre-Audit Corrective Actions, did not start in September as planned. Task 20, Registration Audit, has started early, and what was scheduled to be completed in October has been completed in September.

Also worth noting is qualitative Task A, which has been strong throughout the project. But Tasks B and C have not been as consistent. Our performance slipped in June and July, when scheduled vacations slowed the project more than anticipated. We recovered in August. The consultant fell behind in July and August, but recovered and was on track in September.

These are the major elements in this ISO 9000 OPPM. This project, though complex, did not require much customization of the OPPM. In one page, with very little variation from the standard format, we were able to convey all the important information upper management would need to know about this project.

As a postscript, O.C. Tanner was certified ISO 9000 compliant on schedule. The auditors' conclusion was that O.C. Tanner's system was not only ISO compliant but was unusually mature and substantially more robust than the typical first-time applicant.

CHAPTER

An Introduction to the A3

TOYOTA'S ONE-SHEET COMMUNICATION TOOL

The A3 is a standardized report developed by Toyota that is now being used by hundreds of companies around the world. The name comes from the size of the sheet of paper on which the report is written—the A3 metric-sized paper. In nonmetric companies, the closest English equivalent is the tabloid-sized paper, 11″ × 17″. See the Appendix for more information on the A3 paper format. The use of this one-page-report format probably originated at Hewlett-Packard in the 1970s.

Mike Collins tells this story about the A3:

I first encountered a form of the A3 when I worked for the American Shizuki Corporation in the eighties. I was amazed at how quickly my mentor, Mr. Yasuhiko

Kajikawa, could detail a problem, its solution, and its implementation on a single sheet of paper. (Mr. Kajikawa is today the global CEO and President of Shizuki.) At the time, I attributed this to his artistic ability to present this information in a series of pictures. The series of pictures, each in its own frame, had much of the appearance of a comic strip. Like a comic strip, it would immediately catch my attention and my interest. It was also easy and fun to read. It was clear and concise. We could very easily talk about his "comic strip," and our communication was much better than when we tried to talk about an idea without an A3, particularly in light of the fact that I did not speak Japanese and his English, although improving, did not always communicate what he wanted to say.

I did not know then that the sheet I was looking at was a form of an A3 and that an A3 was an important and very carefully developed report. My thought at that time was that Mr. Kajikawa was very good at sketching things out in a matter of minutes with a paper and pencil. As time passed, I was surprised that many of the Japanese engineers could do this and decided that they must somehow learn to do this in their grade schools. It was only later that I learned that I was looking at a form of an A3, a report created at and used by Toyota. I soon learned that I could construct the same excellent report once I understood the philosophy behind the practice and the method of the practice. I have not gotten as good as my Japanese friends are at sketching out an A3, but I can create a good, concise, interesting, and very informative A3 report on a single sheet of paper.

The report is typically written on a single side of this piece of paper. A strong and beneficial element of the A3 report is the heavy use of graphics: pictures, graphs, illustrations, and so forth, in lieu of a lot of verbiage. Although some A3s are now being written at the desktop computer, the better practice has been to handwrite the A3. The practice of handwriting the A3 makes its usage available to those who are not computer literate and those who do not have computer access. Most importantly, handwriting the A3 is easily done at the point of the problem and at any point in time and space.

More important than the paper size or the means used to write the report is the A3 method: the Deming cycle and the scientific method.

THE DEMING CYCLE

The Deming cycle is named after Dr. W. Edwards Deming. It is a simple sequence of four steps that are fundamental to the successful execution of any initiative: Plan, Do, Check, and Act, or PDCA.

We all want to get things done, and in our rush to do so we are prone to skipping or to giving minimal attention to the Planning step. Before we Do, when we know or think we know what we want to Do, Planning seems to be a costly misuse of time. Later, after or sometimes as we work our way through the execution of what we want to Do, we very often ask ourselves why we didn't take more time to Plan. As we rush through the Do step, we often fail to Check our results to see if we are on track and to see if our objectives are being met. Have you seen or experienced these problems in the execution of an initiative or project? These and many other problems like these seem to plague our projects and initiatives.

The OPPM and the A3 are tools that will help us to avoid fatal flaws like the ones we have mentioned as we execute an initiative or project. In every well- written A3, we will see one or more iterations of the PDCA cycle. At O.C. Tanner we have found that successful project and initiative outcomes are very highly correlated to well-written OPPMs and A3s. As you learn to use these tools, you will realize the same benefits that we have realized.

THE SCIENTIFIC METHOD

The reader should not be put off by the phrase *scientific method*. The scientific method is simply a title for the best problem-solving practice that the world has at this time. You do not have to be a certified scientist to understand, apply, and benefit from learning to use the scientific method.

In fact, most of us often use the scientific method in our everyday activities. For example, most of us have made toast. Let's say that your new toaster has a temperature setting of 1 to 10. The first time you made toast, you studied the toaster manual and decided that a setting of 5 would make your toast just the way you like it. You set the toaster at 5, inserted the bread, and waited. When the toaster finished, you observed that the toast was not as well done as you wanted. The next time, you adjusted the setting to 7. This time the toast was too dark. After making your toast several times, you determined that a setting of just past 6 would give you perfect toast every time.

This is the scientific method of problem-solving. First, we study a given situation. Then, based on our study, we make a decision. In the verbiage of science, this is our hypothesis: We believe 5 is the right setting. Next, we test our decision through experimentation. Based on our experiments, we then come to a conclusion. If we are satisfied with our conclusion, we then make a change or changes to reflect what we have learned. If we are not satisfied with the results, then we make an adjustment to our process or our thinking and complete another round of experimentation, that is, we try the toast at a different setting.

The steps of the scientific method are normally defined in scientific terms, such as hypothesis, analysis, etc. At the O.C. Tanner Company, where 63 percent of our people speak English as a second language, it was necessary to find simpler words that non-native English speakers could more quickly learn and understand.

We constructed what we call the STEPS model. STEPS is a very meaningful acronym for See–Think–Experiment–Prove–Sustain. Throughout this book we will use the STEPS model whenever a scientific method story line is required as in the case of solving a problem.

THE A3 STORY LINE

A key underpinning of the A3 is that it tells a story in a very complete, concise, and factual manner. It is somewhat parallel to the oath sworn in a court of law: Do you promise to tell the truth, the whole truth, and nothing but the truth? Through the PDCA cycle and the scientific method (STEPS), the A3 helps us to tell the right story, the whole story, and nothing but the most pertinent facts of the story. The story line not only helps us to create a succinct, readable, and interesting executive report, it guides our thinking throughout the execution of our project or initiative.

What is the story that it tells? The A3 is used to tell any number of different stories. The A3 is used to define and communicate business strategy. It is used to define and communicate a problem to be solved, the steps of solving the problem, possible solutions to the problem, the testing of the proposed solutions, and the implementation of the final solution.

The story line may vary somewhat, based on the story being told. If we are using the A3 for strategy deployment, the A3 story line will tend to strongly reflect the PDCA cycle. If the A3 is being used to solve a problem, the story line will be that of the scientific method (STEPS).

Although there are many applications of the A3, this book will focus on the use of the two most common uses of the A3: the deployment/execution of strategy and problem-solving. These two applications are closely related in that the execution of every strategy will most often require the solving of many problems. The A3s presented in this book are about the execution of strategy—getting it done.

A SAMPLE A3

Figure 4.1 on pages 58–59 presents an A3. The details of the A3 are discussed in the following chapters.

DESCRIPTON & PRIMARY OBJECTIVE

Optimize gumming process, by reducing time in the gum oven by 50%.

SEE—BACKGROUND

Gumming is the process of covering the background, or unpolished surfaces of an emblem, with a gum-type substance. It is meant to protect these unpolished surfaces from being hit or polished during the polishing process. The gum has to be cured in an oven before polishing and is washed away after the final buffing. It is a non-value added process.

SEE—CURRENT CONDITION

Ovens are set at 200 degrees, and 8 minutes for optimal gum curing.

THINK—OBJECTIVES

Reduce time in the oven to at least 4 minutes (50%)

THINK—COUNTERMEASURES

Find the optimal time/temperature combination that will reduce time spent in the oven. Use Six Sigma as a tool for this improvement

EXPERIMENT—PROGRESS

We needed to determine a response. (how we measure if gum is cured). Gum is a mixture that includes water, the % of moisture loss, would become a good response.

We did a hardness test to prove that as the % moisture loss increased, the hardness/strength of the gum would increase. (*There is a positive correlation.*)

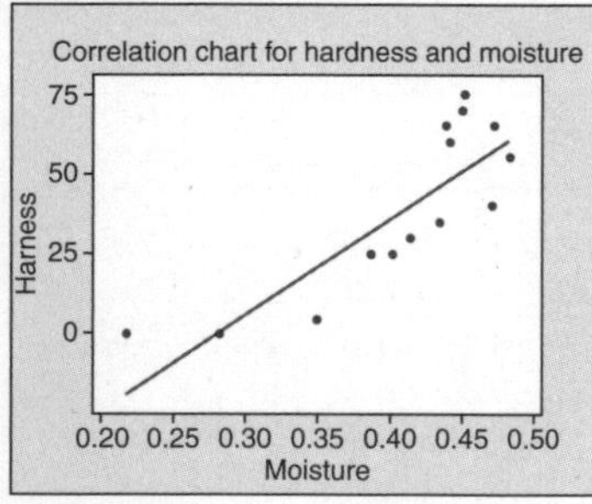

<u>% of moisture loss was calculated by</u>:

1. Finding emblem dry weight
2. Weighing the emblem after gum was applied.
3. Finding the difference (gum weight 1)
4. Weighing emblem after being in the oven
5. Subtracting that from the emblem dry wt. (gum weight 2)
6. Dividing gum wt. 2 into gum wt. 1(%) e.g:

Emblem weight		gum weight 1
After gum	dry	(difference)
0.340	0.300	0.040

Emblem weight		gum weight 2
After oven	dry	(difference)
0.325	0.300	0.025

gum weight 2 divided into gum weight 1	
% moist. Loss=	62.5%

Hardness was determined with a durometer.

We wanted to pick a range for the oven temperature and started at 400, 375, 350, 275, 260 and 250 degrees. We found these settings were to hot for the gum. The results were bubbly and flaky gum. The ovens can fluctuate 10 degrees, so we selected our highest temperature at 230 degrees. (*if we picked 240, it could vary enough to reach 250 degrees, which is our limit*).
We picked 130 degrees as our lower value, this would allow us to see a wide range.

In our **screening** experiment showed that there is not a lot of variation in the process. We tested all factors that could effect the gum process and determined that time, temperature, and emblem were all significant factors.

<u>Factor</u>	<u>Type</u>	<u>Levels</u>	<u>Values</u>
Temp	fixed	2	130, 230 (*degrees*)
Time	fixed	2	2, 8 (*minutes*)
Gum	fixed	2	New, Old
Emblem	fixed	2	Deep, Shallow

The emblem factor is beyond our control. So we decided to optimize the process, based on a time and temperature that would work for all.

<u>Factor</u>	<u>Type</u>	<u>Levels</u>	<u>Values</u>
Time	fixed	3	3, 4, 5
Temp	fixed	3	200, 220, 240
Emblem2	fixed	3	1, 2, 3 (*different depths*)

EXPERIMENT-REVIEW

Discovered that 235 degrees at 4 minutes is best
Best run: 240 degrees for 3 - 4 minutes
Worst run: 200 degrees for 3 minutes
Best predicted: 235 degrees for 4 minutes
Worst predicted: 200 degrees for 3 minutes
Center: 220 degrees for 3.5 minutes
Six Sigma testing complete.

PROVE-SUCCESS MEASURES

Gum ovens were changed too 235 degrees for 4 minutes curing time. After these changes were made, Angels and Magic had some bubbling issues. Further testing showed that the temperatures in the drawers varied from top to bottom. Sometimes in a 30–40 degree swing. The reason for this was that every oven was a built just a little bit different. Also, the design of the oven didn't encourage a consistent temperature.

FIGURE 4.1 *An A3*

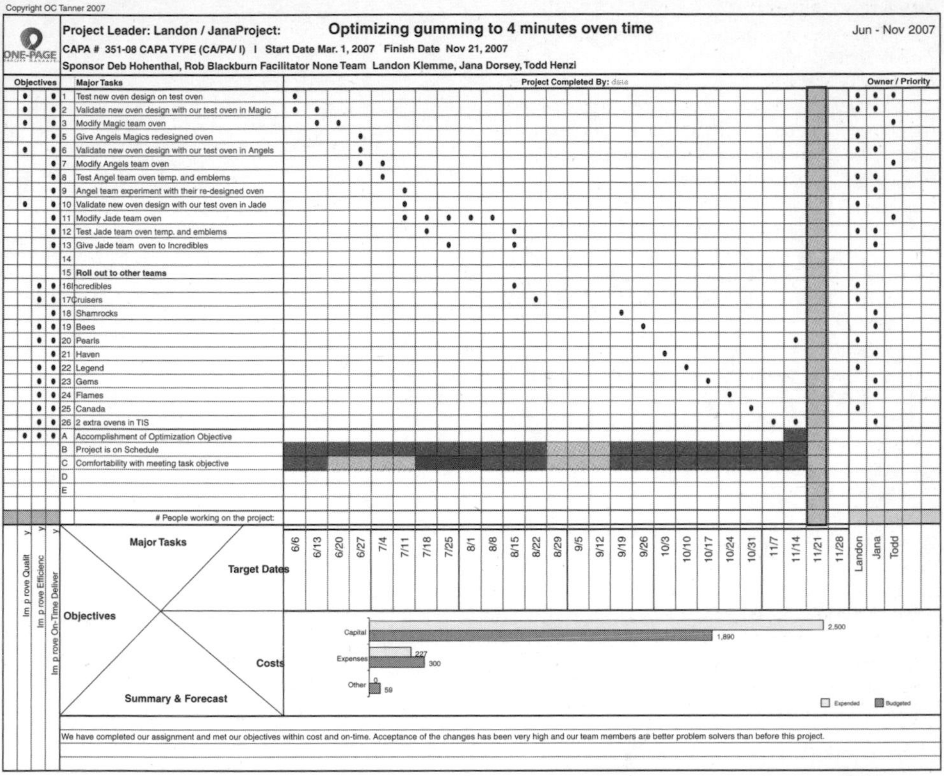

ONE-PAGE

Project Leader: Landon / JanaProject: **Optimizing gumming to 4 minutes oven time** Jun - Nov 2007

CAPA # 351-08 CAPA TYPE (CA/PA/ I) I Start Date Mar. 1, 2007 Finish Date Nov 21, 2007

Sponsor Deb Hohenthal, Rob Blackburn Facilitator None Team Landon Klemme, Jana Dorsey, Todd Henzi

Objectives | Major Tasks | Project Completed By: | Owner / Priority

Im p rove Qualit y	Im p rove Efficienc y	Im p rove On-Time Deliver y		Major Tasks	6/6	6/13	6/20	6/27	7/4	7/11	7/18	7/25	8/1	8/8	8/15	8/22	8/29	9/5	9/12	9/19	9/26	10/3	10/10	10/17	10/24	10/31	11/7	11/14	11/21	11/28	Landon	Jana	Todd
•		•	1	Test new oven design on test oven	•																										•	•	•
•		•	2	Validate new oven design with our test oven in Magic	•	•																									•	•	
•		•	3	Modify Magic team oven		•	•																										•
		•	5	Give Angels Magics redesigned oven				•																							•		
•		•	6	Validate new oven design with our test oven in Angels				•																							•	•	
		•	7	Modify Angels team oven				•	•																								•
		•	8	Test Angel team oven temp. and emblems					•																						•	•	
		•	9	Angel team experiment with their re-designed oven						•																						•	
•		•	10	Validate new oven design with our test oven in Jade						•																					•		
		•	11	Modify Jade team oven						•	•	•	•	•																			•
		•	12	Test Jade team oven temp. and emblems							•				•																•	•	
		•	13	Give Jade team oven to Incredibles								•			•																	•	
			14																														
			15	**Roll out to other teams**																													
	•	•	16	Incredibles											•																•		
	•	•	17	Cruisers												•															•		
		•	18	Shamrocks																•												•	
	•	•	19	Bees																	•											•	
	•	•	20	Pearls																								•			•		
		•	21	Haven																		•										•	
	•	•	22	Legend																			•								•		
	•	•	23	Gems																				•								•	
	•	•	24	Flames																					•							•	
	•	•	25	Canada																						•					•		
	•	•	26	2 extra ovens in TIS																							•	•				•	
•	•	•	A	Accomplishment of Optimization Objective																													
			B	Project is on Schedule																													
			C	Comfortability with meeting task objective																													
			D																														
			E																														
				# People working on the project:																													

Major Tasks | Target Dates | Objectives | Costs | Summary & Forecast

	Expended	Budgeted
Capital	2,500	1,890
Expenses	227	300
Other	0	59

We have completed our assignment and met our objectives within cost and on-time. Acceptance of the changes has been very high and our team members are better problem solvers than before this project.

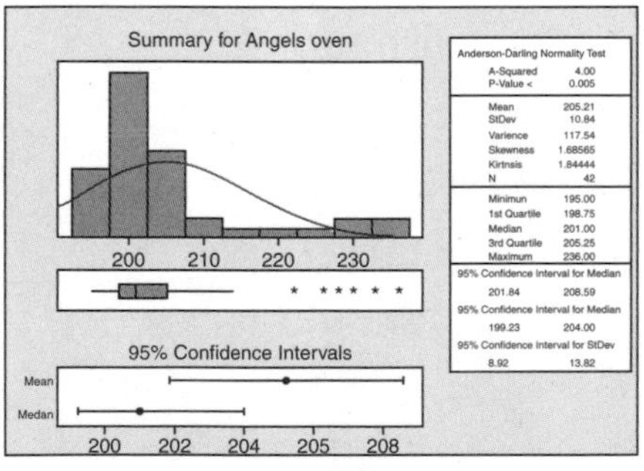

SEE—Current oven condition

Outside air brought in by side-mounted fan.

Air directed onto heating coil. Heat moves up and through 3 holes at the top

THINK—In talking with Todd Henzi. It made sense for us to close off the top holes, eliminate the outside air, and mount an internal fan.

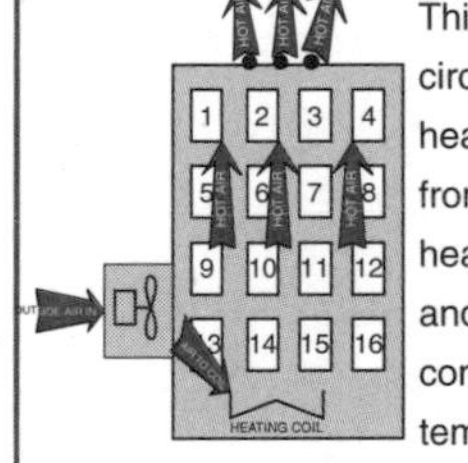

This fan will circulate the heat coming from the heating coil, and create a consistent temperature among the drawers.

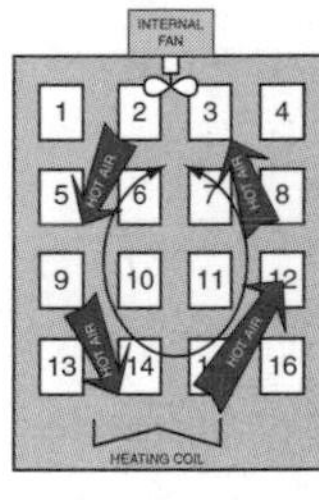

EXPERIMENT—Testing the drawers did show a consistency. A difference of 5-8 degrees on AVG.

PROVE-MEASUREABLES—This new design was tested in the Angels & Magic teams for 3 weeks. No complaints were noted. Feedback was given about the consistency of the cured gum by team members in both teams.

SUSTAIN (Best Practices-Review-Migrate)—All emblematic teams have a newly redesigned oven. No other training was necessary. Objectives have been met and sustained.

FIGURE 4.1 *(Continued)*

CHAPTER

OPPM/A3 for ISO 9000

In this chapter, we bring the OPPM and the A3 together into a simple and very powerful document and tool for execution. We call the combination of these two documents an OPPM/A3.

As a teaching example, we will use the efforts of the O.C. Tanner Company to achieve ISO registration.

The objective of this chapter is to present the basic elements and use of an A3. It is by no means an exhaustive treatise on this subject. By the end of this chapter, the person who is not familiar with an A3 should have learned the following:

1. How to construct and write an OPPM/A3.
2. How OPPM/A3s help our people to become better at executing strategy—getting it done.
3. How OPPM/A3s help us to be better communicators and more successful leaders.
4. The simplicity and power of the A3 report.

CONSTRUCTING AN OPPM/A3

Whether using metric-size A3 paper or English-size tabloid paper for our OPPM/A3, we fold our OPPM/A3s in half so that they open and read much like a newspaper. We almost always arrange each half of the OPPM/A3 into two newspaper-like columns.

We try to keep our information on a single side of the paper, although we sometimes find that more involved projects, problem-solving efforts, and improvements are better described by using both sides. This may be because we are still learning to be more succinct and focused in the expression of our thoughts. The first effort should always be to use a single side only. A graphical depiction of this format is given in Figure 5.1.

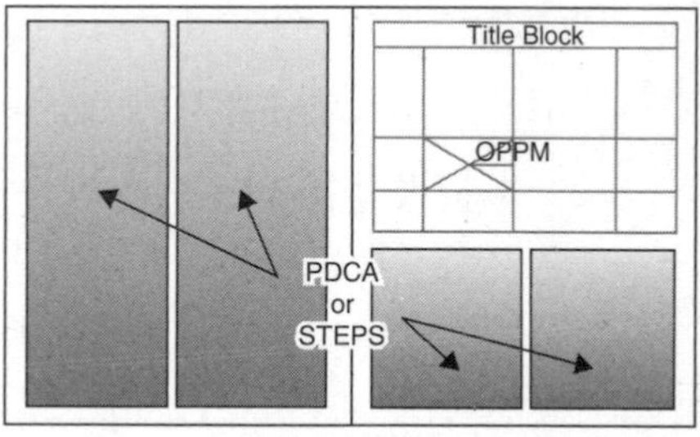

FIGURE 5.1 *OPPM/A3 Template*

When deploying strategy, we use a PDCA story line (Figure 5.2).

And when solving problems, we use a STEPS story line (Figure 5.3).

Note that the title block of the OPPM becomes the title block of the A3 as well. In keeping with Lean principles, we do not want to duplicate information with both an A3 title block and an OPPM title block.

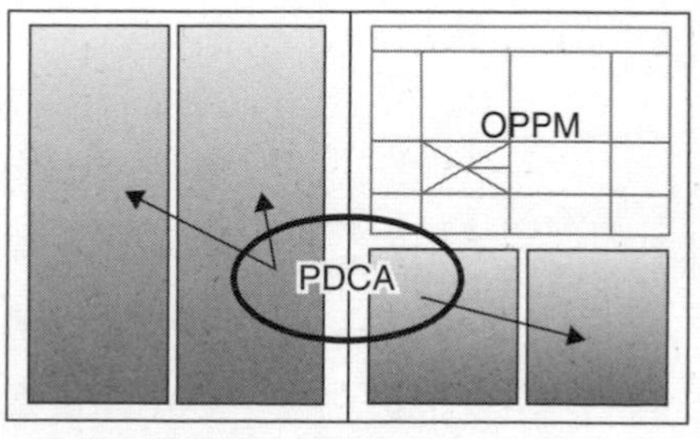

FIGURE 5.2 *OPPM/A3 Template with a PDCA Story Line*

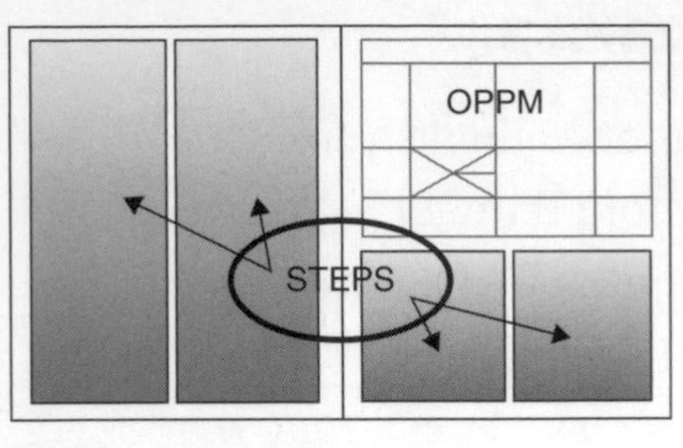

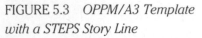

FIGURE 5.3 *OPPM/A3 Template with a STEPS Story Line*

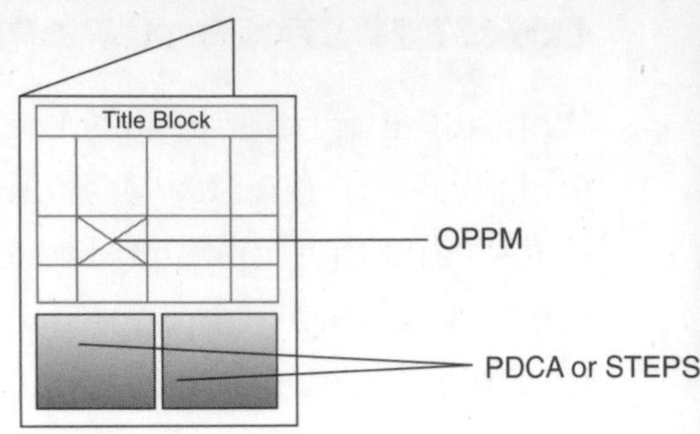

FIGURE 5.4 *Folded OPPM/A3*

When folded, the single sheet of paper has the appearance of a small newspaper (Figure 5.4).

We often insert other *supporting* documents when needed, such as research and experimentation data and details into this folded OPPM/A3, using it as a file folder. The OPPM/A3 itself includes only summary data as needed for an executive report, not supporting research, experimentation data, and project details.

To protect the OPPM/A3 and to keep supporting documents together with the OPPM/A3, we often insert the OPPM/A3 into a one-half or one-third cut file folder (Figure 5.5).

FIGURE 5.5 *Folded OPPM/A3 in Half-Cut File Folder*

Note that the OPPM/A3 has the title bar to the front in this folder, making the subject of the OPPM/A3 readily visible. The OPPM/A3 itself is our report to management and any other interested parties. It is also the managing document for the project or initiative. The entire file is a working and living document set used throughout the OPPM/A3 effort.

PLAN—DO—CHECK—ACT (PDCA)

In this chapter, we use as an illustrating example of an OPPM/A3 our ISO registration effort at O.C. Tanner. PDCA is an appropriate story line for this OPPM/A3 registration effort because it was a strategic initiative for a desired improvement and not an effort directed at solving a specific problem.

To help those who are not familiar with PDCA, we next present some additional understanding of the PDCA cycle. Those who are already familiar with PDCA may choose to skip this discussion.

Plan—Do—Check—Act, or PDCA, is a method of continuous improvement. It has been made very popular by Dr. W. Edward Deming and through its use in the Toyota system.

The first step of the PDCA cycle is Plan (Figure 5.6).

The Plan step includes the definition of an improvement. This could be the resolution of a problem, the testing of an idea, or some other desired change. In the Plan step, the situation is defined, studied, and analyzed. Team members drill down to the root cause of the problem and then seek to determine the most creative approaches and the best possible solutions to the problem. The final effort of the Plan step is the development of the plan schedule.

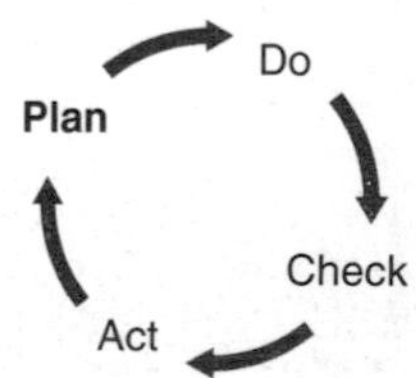

FIGURE 5.6
Plan–Do–Check–Act Cycle

The OPPM in the OPPM/A3 is the plan. The OPPM gives everyone involved, as well as those who are watching, a clear definition of where the effort is headed. It communicates time frame, who is involved, progress, and what is to be done. The benefit is the alignment and focus of everyone involved.

The A3 portion of the OPPM/A3 Plan section is the reasoning behind the plan, including other countermeasures considered. It also communicates the need and the justification for this improvement. The benefit is the building of buy-in, as well as the creative or thinking participation of all who are involved with, associated with, or in some way affected by the desired improvement.

The second step of the PDCA cycle is Do (Figure 5.7).

Do is the execution of the plan. The OPPM captures and visually communicates the progress being made, and it graphically depicts performance to target. The OPPM becomes a tool by which all of those involved, including management, can note and respond to exceptions and variations to plan.

The A3 portion of Do captures the learning that occurs as the plan is executed. What is working and what is not working? Why? What adjustments are we making and why? Remember as you write the A3 that you are writing a report, not just for today, but for future audiences as well. In the future, others can learn from our mistakes and build upon our successes. They cannot do this if they are unaware of our experiences. The A3 captures this learning. It also provides management

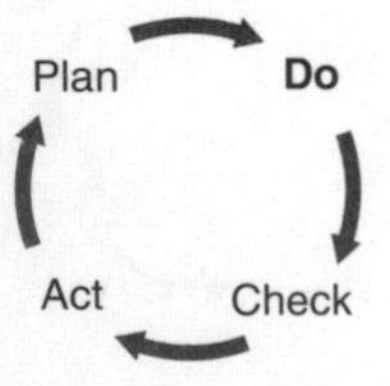

FIGURE 5.7
Plan–Do–Check–Act Cycle

with a clear understanding of why the effort is proceeding as it is.

The third step of the PDCA cycle is Check (Figure 5.8).

FIGURE 5.8
Plan–Do–Check–Act Cycle

In this step, results of the planned effort are analyzed to review and confirm that the planned objectives and targets have been reached and that the planned effort has actually accomplished the intent of the strategy. The meaning of the word *check* as used in the PDCA cycle, can be better understood by replacing it with the word *study*. Now is the time to reflect and ask ourselves if we are truly on course and if we could or should be doing more. This thinking and our conclusions are captured in the A3 and are invaluable to those who, in the future, may be making the same or a similar effort.

The next step in the cycle is Act (Figure 5.9).

When we find in the Check step that we have not accomplished all that we intended to accomplish or that the outcomes are not as expected, then we must Act upon that information and make the necessary adjustments to bring our effort back on track or to elevate our efforts to a point that the desired objectives are accomplished.

We should learn from our failures, realizing that it is through failure that most learning occurs. The A3 content of the OPPM/A3 should capture this learning.

FIGURE 5.9
Plan–Do–Check–Act Cycle

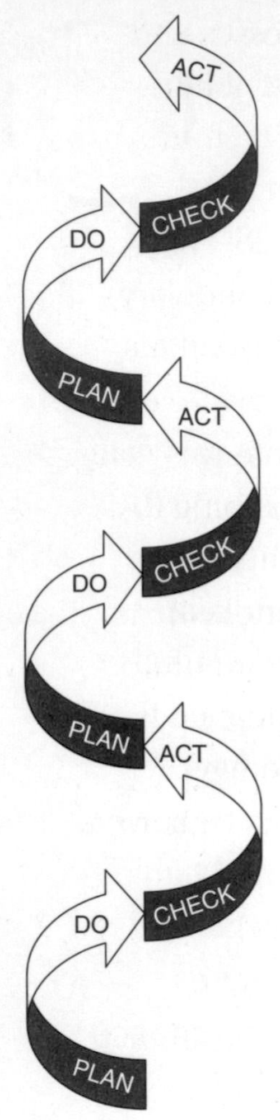

FIGURE 5.10 *The Continuous Improvement Cycle of PDCA*

This is one important way in which the A3 will prove to be invaluable.

When we find, in the Check step, that our efforts have accomplished all that we intended, then there are at least two specific elements of the Act step. First, make sure that all of the appropriate thinking, learning, and results have been captured in the OPPM/A3 and then present it to other appropriate parties in the organization to propagate the learning throughout the organization. Second, ask what the next effort or improvement should be and begin that PDCA cycle. This is in the spirit of continuous improvement. One PDCA cycle leads to the next (see Figure 5.10).

AN OPPM/A3 ISO REGISTRATION EFFORT

At the O.C. Tanner Company, we had been involved in the transformation of the company to Lean for several years. In 2003 our sales people asked that we pursue ISO registration because they felt it was necessary for our international expansion and that ISO registration had become a necessary competitive weapon in our marketplace.

We had in place many well-defined processes and systems. The ISO requirements used a different language and we felt that in many ways the ISO requirements would force us to undo years of effort. The challenge then became one of pursuing the ISO registration without undoing years of very good and very successful work. The ISO registration effort also came at a time when our Lean momentum was really beginning to accelerate and we did not want to lose this gain. Furthermore, it appeared to us that we were going to have to put in place many additional documents and processes—the opposite of our direction with Lean. Nevertheless, our corporate leadership decided that obtaining ISO registration was of such significance that it should be an element of our corporate strategy.

Note that ISO registration is not a problem to be solved; although there were problems associated with obtaining registration, it is a strategic initiative. As a strategic initiative, a PDCA story line was the best fit:

- Plan the accomplishment of the initiative
- Do or execute the plan
- Check the results
- Act upon discrepancies to plan as we progress and determine what our next improvement effort should be.

THE TITLE BLOCK

We began our construction of the OPPM/A3 with a simple title block in the OPPM.

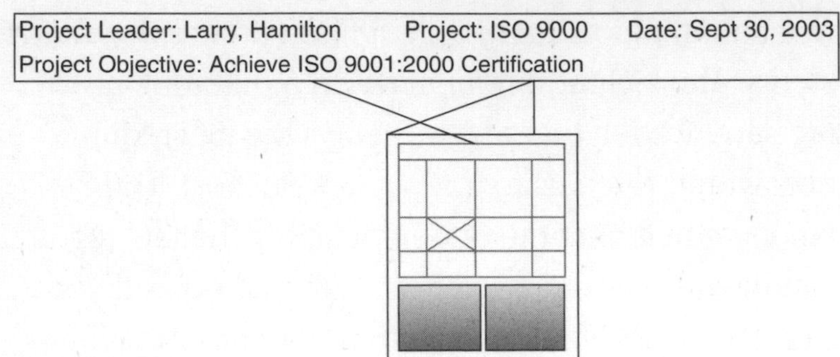

FIGURE 5.11 *OPPM/A3 ISO Registration Title Block*

Note: The Project Objective should have been ISO 9001:2000 registration. We didn't know at the time that ISO does not grant a certification but rather registration.

The project name or problem descriptor, along with the management sponsor, the team facilitator, team member names, and pertinent dates, can appear in the title block.

Our title block for the ISO registration initiative is shown in Figure 5.11.

A good A3 report generally includes six elements in the Plan step:

1. A background statement
2. A current state condition
3. A root cause analysis
4. A future state (target) condition
5. Countermeasures
6. An implementation plan

Plan—Background Statement

It is with the background statement that our OPPM/A3 story for ISO registration begins. The story begins at the far left hand side of 11″ 17″ tabloid-size paper (Figure 5.12).

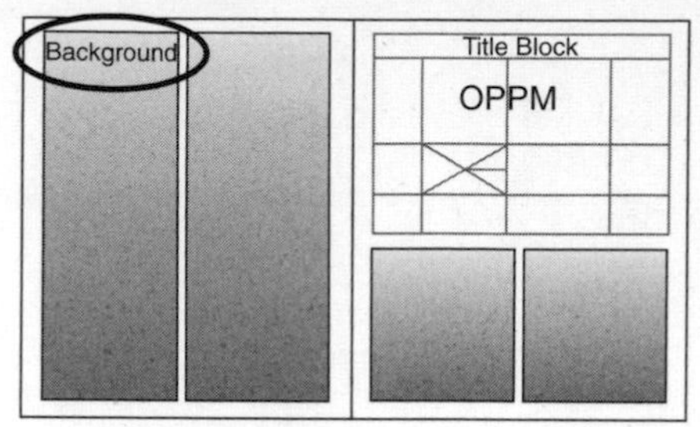

FIGURE 5.12 *OPPM/A3 ISO Registration Template*

The background statement should include a succinct history leading up to the problem and a clear statement of the problem. Our background statement in our ISO registration OPPM/A3 was very simple:

- We do not have a previous history with ISO.
- The need for ISO registration has been determined by our customers. We have in fact, lost a great customer (a major chemical manufacturer) because of our lack of ISO registration. Our lack of ISO registration is being used by our competitors as a competitive weapon against us, even though we are the clear front-runner with the best quality in our industry.
- We need ISO registration to do business in foreign countries.

Figure 5.13 shows how the Background Statement appeared in our OPPM/A3.

Outlining the background and history of our ISO registration need was an excellent way of building a common understanding and vision of the task at hand.

Background

Our competitors have begun to use our lack of an ISO registration as a weapon against us. We recently lost a competitive bid for this very reason.

We have initiated efforts to more aggressively expand our international market. As we do so it is becoming increasingly important for us to have ISO certification. Without ISO certification, it will not be possible for us to achieve significant market presence in most foreign countries.

Although we are without any previous ISO experience, our objective is to achieve ISO certification by year end.

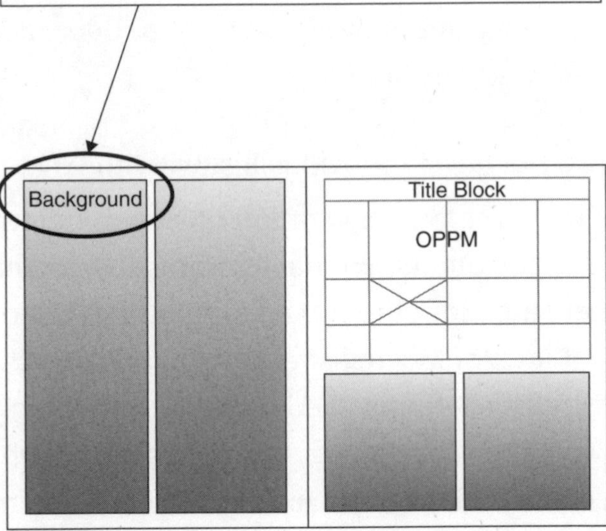

FIGURE 5.13 *OPPM/A3 ISO Registration Background Statement*

Plan—Current State Condition

The next element of Plan is a realistic and definitive statement of the current conditions. This will often be a significant effort of study and research that may include data collection, value stream mapping, surveying, observation, measurement, and so forth. Because this statement will be the baseline against which future improvement is measured, it is important that this statement or at least the key elements of the statement be measureable.

In our ISO registration effort, our lack of any knowledge about ISO made this a significant and time-consuming effort. We needed to learn everything about ISO that we possibly could and in the shortest time period possible. One critical item quickly rose to the surface. Among our 1,600 employees there was not anyone with any significant ISO experience. We had little understanding of its requirements or what we needed to do to achieve ISO registration. We were even uncertain about the process required to apply for ISO registration. Clearly, we needed some outside help, and we decided to search for a very qualified ISO consultant or consultant group.

Once we found and obtained the services of an ISO consultant, we discovered very quickly that we needed to thoroughly audit our existing processes and systems to find how we compared to the ISO standard and thereby establish a baseline for our initiative efforts.

We also discovered that the registration process required us to enlist the services of an ISO registrar.

Note in the preceding statements that the self-auditing and the need for outside expertise early on in the consideration of ISO registration were learning processes. This learning, captured in the OPPM/A3, will help other O.C. Tanner companies as they pursue the ISO registration.

The Current State Condition appeared in our OPPM/A3 as shown in Figure 5.14.

Current State Condition

From our initial review of ISO, its requirements, and the application process, and in view of the short time frame available to us, it is clear what we need some outside assistance. Within our ranks, we do not have anyone with sufficient ISO experience to guide us through this process. We have decided that a critical element of our effort to be successful in accomplishing this strategic initiative is the acquisition of an experienced ISO consultant. The need for a consultant is immediate in that we find we are not able to complete the PLAN phase without this assistance. We initiated a search and have enlisted the services of ███ ████ ██████, ██. We will also need to acquire the services of an ISO registrar. It is through the registrar that the ISO registration process is completed. We will use the services of our ISO consultant to help us identify an appropriate ISO Registrar.

The details of our ISO pre-audit assessment are found in the ISO Audit Summary (attached). To summarize, we have found that for the most part we have in place everything needed to meet ISO registration requirements. We do need to change some of our language and we need to provide our people with a significant amount of training to help them understand the ISO requirements and language. We will also need to make a number of other minor changes to be compliant.

Our workloads will increase as we work our way through this and we will need to be very aware of schedule in order to meet our dates.

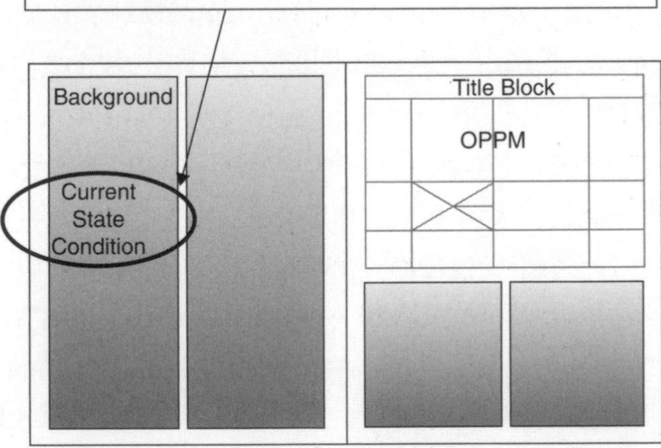

FIGURE 5.14 *OPPM/A3 ISO Registration Current State Condition*

The team next began collecting information about ISO to help them clearly see and understand not only the problem or project but also to help them begin to see possible solutions to our Lean-ISO concerns. It is very important that the team determine for themselves the exact problem and its extent rather than accepting without question the statements of others about the nature of the problem or project.

As our team began to investigate the requirements of ISO, they began to realize that not all the requirements were going to be as difficult to meet as originally thought. With each study of the requirements came a clearer understanding of the ISO language and a clearer understanding of the broadness of the task at hand. This was the beginning of team engagement.

The Current Condition Statement often includes quality, cost and delivery data, pareto charts, Ishikawa diagrams, and so forth. The Current Condition Statements may also include the current state value stream map. Current Condition Statements should provide sufficient detail to clearly define the current state, but they should also be succinct. Visuals and graphics can be very helpful and are very much encouraged.

An important aspect of the A3 is its power to communicate. It is a good practice at this point in the A3 process to begin distributing copies to all who may be affected by the changes that will come as result of the team's efforts. Often the A3s are enlarged to poster size and posted on easel tripods located in highly visible employee areas and in the area to be affected by the team's efforts. Along with the posters, signage is posted requesting feedback from all who may be concerned. Sticky notes and felt-tip markers are left at the easel to facilitate the feedback.

Plan—Root Cause Analysis

Root Cause Analysis is the practice of drilling down on a problem until the real source of the problem is identified. Too often we accept, carte blanche, the statement of a problem without making any effort to determine if the statement is at all correct. Very often, what is stated as a problem is not the problem at all but the symptom of an underlying problem. There are many approaches to Root Cause Analysis: 5 Why's, Kepner-Tregoe Problem Analysis, Pareto Analysis, Fault Tree Analysis, Ishikawa Diagrams, and so forth, which can and should be used to find the real problem.

In our ISO registration effort, we were not solving a problem per se, but rather establishing a new practice. As such, we left Root Cause Analysis out of our OPPM/A3.

Plan—Future State (Target) Condition

As a team develops a clear understanding of the problem or effort at hand, they will generally also begin to develop a good understanding of what the ideal condition should be. At this point, the team can set objectives and goals for their work effort. These should be reviewed with the sponsor and other leaders associated with the problem. The development of consensus is generally accomplished in a short meeting between the team and those concerned. The agenda of the meeting is a statement of the problem, a summary of the current condition, and a statement of the proposed objectives and target condition. The objective of the meeting is consensus that the team's direction and objectives are aligned with corporate direction and needs. This clearer understanding of the team's direction and objectives deepens team engagement.

With the competitive pressure we were feeling and in light of our effort to expand internationally, we agreed that we needed the ISO registration sooner rather than later. We set a target date of having our ISO registration in hand by January 2004. This Future State Target Condition was then added to the OPPM/A3 and appeared as shown in Figure 5.15.

The A3s previously distributed and posted in strategic locations of the company were updated with the Future State Target Condition. It is important to note, however, that very careful thought must be given to these statements before they are posted. Many statements can be interpreted to mean a reduction of force. It may be a good idea to meet with all those concerned before posting this information to clearly communicate the exact intention of the team. If a reduction of personnel in a specific area is the objective, then it is necessary to also communicate the assignments to which these people will be moved as well as how they will be prepared for the new assignments.

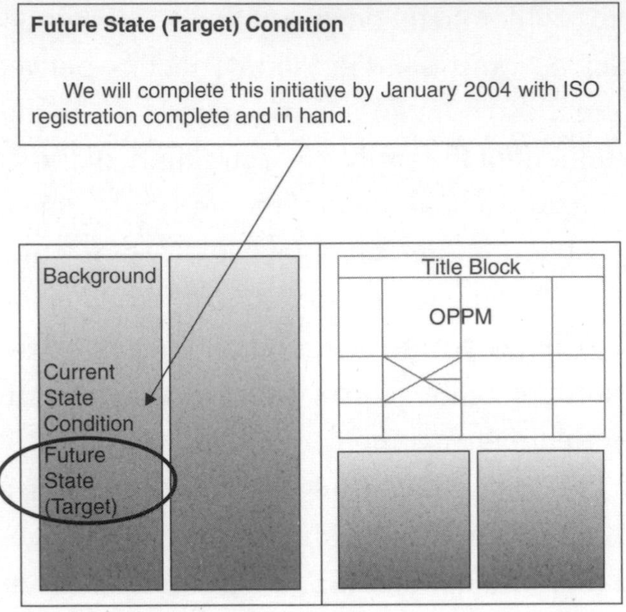

FIGURE 5.15 *OPPM/A3 ISO Registration Future State (Target) Condition*

Plan—Countermeasures or Proposed Actions

Countermeasures are developed through much analysis and brainstorming. Countermeasures are the approaches that will be taken to resolve a problem or, as in this instance, to complete an initiative. The word *solution* implies finality, which is contrary to the spirit of Lean—that is, the spirit that there is always opportunity to improve. The Lean world has, therefore, adopted Toyota's usage of the word *countermeasure* so as not to imply that a given tool, process, or system cannot be improved upon.

Countermeasures are almost always written as a statement of hypothesis followed by a statement of the experiment. For example, a countermeasure to being overweight could be:

If I reduce my calorie intake by 400 calories a day, I will lose one pound a week. I will do this for ten weeks, and during this time period I should lose 10 pounds.

This might work. We don't know. We will know at the end of the ten-week trial period. At the end of the period we will check the result, and if the result is not as expected, we will make a change to the experiment. One can see, in this type of a statement, a PDCA cycle. Good countermeasures have built-in PDCA cycles.

Countermeasures must be clearly communicated to all parties concerned. Additionally, it is a final opportunity and invitation for all concerns and any recently developed ideas to be communicated to the team before the implementation phase begins. The objective is to develop consensus among all of those involved with or affected by the proposed countermeasures.

In the case of our ISO registration effort, we asked ourselves what steps were needed to be successful in completing this initiative. There were many needed steps, but as we organized the steps into a sequence, we found four fairly distinct groups of steps that we called phases: Definition Phase, Implementation Phase, Verification Phase, and Validation Phase. These phases became the high-level countermeasures about which we organized all of our efforts (Figure 5.16).

Countermeasures

Definition Phase – We have much of what ISO requires already in place. However, it is not organized as a corporate quality manual. This will require a team to lead and a cross-function effort.

Implementation Phase – As we publish our quality manual, we will need to give special attention to training our people in its use as well as the usage of new ISO-required forms and work instructions.

Verification Phase – Before making application for ISO registration, we will need to conduct several self-audits and management reviews.

Validation Phase – Apply for ISO registration.

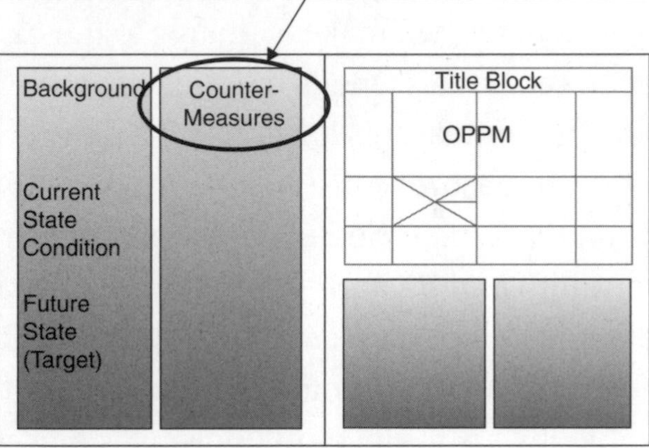

FIGURE 5.16 *OPPM/A3 ISO Registration Countermeasures Statement*

Plan—Implementation

In most A3s, this section is used to present the plan for implementation of the changes. The plan includes the schedule for each event, who is responsible for each aspect of the implementation, and other details.

When we combine the A3 and the OPPM, we can in this section reduce the presentation to a high level overview—a brief synopsis or outline of the implementation plan—and leave the details to the OPPM. The OPPM then presents the details of the plan—the whats, the whos, the whens, the plan progress, and other information in a more detailed and correlated view. The A3 implementation section is left to present a quick read or overview of the plan, and the OPPM provides the details of the implementation, should the reader want the details, particularly with respect to plan progress. The use of the OPPM in an A3 presents far more information than what is generally included in an A3. The OPPM is presented on the right top side of the OPPM/A3.

The OPPM for our ISO registration initiative was described in the Chapter 3. In our ISO registration OPPM/A3, we added only a brief high-level statement about the plan and left the details to the OPPM (Figure 5.17).

Be sure to update the posted and distributed OPPM/A3s as the implementation plan progresses. This practice keeps everyone in the loop and continues to build buy-in.

DO

Do is the second step of the PDCA cycle. It is the execution of our plan. The OPPM is our plan of execution and is used daily throughout the implementation period to guide our management effort. It provides us with the high-level information that we need to know and also gives us what needs to be done day by day throughout the initiative or project. It tells us who has leadership responsibility and who else is involved in each step of the plan. It provides us with a track record of how we

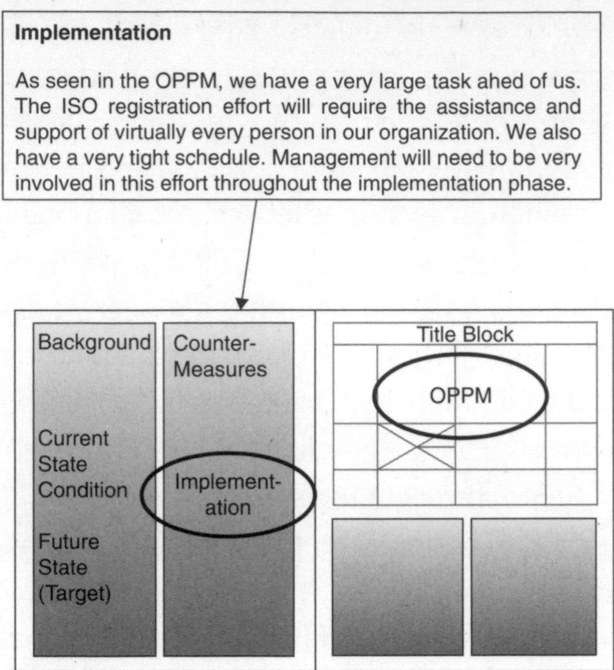
Implementation
As seen in the OPPM, we have a very large task ahed of us. The ISO registration effort will require the assistance and support of virtually every person in our organization. We also have a very tight schedule. Management will need to be very involved in this effort throughout the implementation phase.
Background
Current State Condition
Future State (Target)
Counter-Measures
Implement-ation
Title Block
OPPM

FIGURE 5.17 *OPPM/A3 ISO Registration Implementation Statement*

have performed to date. Most importantly, it gives to everyone this same clear understanding of who, what, where, and when.

It is interesting to note that when plans are clearly communicated and all are engaged and aligned, we are often able to exceed our expectations. Our ISO registration effort began as a difficult and daunting task, particularly in light of several other significant efforts under way at the time. Even so, with good planning and a clear vision, we exceeded our expectation and received ISO registration almost a month ahead of time. The significance of this is even greater when we look

ONE-PAGE

Project Leader: Larry Hamilton | **Project: ISO 9000** | Date: Sept 30

Project Objective: Achieve ISO 9001:2000 Certificaton

Organizational Commitment	Develop Quality Manual	Develop Procedures	Develop Work Instructions	Develop Records	Develop Internal Audit System	#	Major Tasks	April	May	June	July	August	September	October	November	December	January	February	Executive Management	Project Manager	ISO Project Teams	Internal Auditors	ISO Consultant
							Definition Phase																
●						1	Establish Development Team	●	●										A	B			
●						2	Train Development Team	●	●											A	B		B
●						3	Develop Process Map	●	●											B			A
●						4	Select Registrar	●	●	●									B	A			
	●	●	●			5	Define Level II Procedures	●	●	●	●									A	B		B
	●	●	●			6	Quality Manual	●	●	●	●								B	B	B		A
			●	●		7	Work Instructions and Forms	●	●	●	●										A		B
		●	●	●	●	8	Records	●	●	●	●										A		
							Implementation Phase																
		●	●	●	●	9	Train New Processes			●	●	●								B	A		B
		●				10	Publish Quality Manual				●	●								A			B
				●		11	New Forms/Work Instructions			●	●										A		B
		●	●			12	Put Procedures under Document Control			●	●									A	B		B
			●			13	Implement Procedures			●	●	●							A	B	B		B
	○	○	○	○	○	14	Awareness Training			●	●	○							B	A			
							Verification Phase																
	●					15	Develop and Train Internal Auditors				●	●										B	A
●	●					16	Implement Internal Auditing Program				●	●							B	B		A	B
	●	●	●	●	●	17	Conduct Management Review				●	●							A	B		B	
	●	●	●	●	●	18	Conduct Pre-Audit Assessment					●	●							B		A	
			○			19	Pre-Audit Corrective Actions						○	○					B	A	B		
							Validation Phase																
○	○	○	○	○	○	20	Registration Audit							●	○					A			B
○		○	○	○	○	21	Corrective Actions							○	○	○			B		A		
○						22	Certification									○	○		A	A	A	A	A
○						23	Project Closeout										○	○		A	B	B	B
●						A	Organizational Commitment												A	B	B	B	B
○	○	○	○	○	○	B	Our Performance												B	A	B	B	B
○	○	○	○	○	○	C	Consultant Performance												B	B	B	B	A
							# Procedures Completed:	1/17	6/17	12/17	17/20	17/19	19/19										

Project Completed By: Feb — Owner/Priority

Major Tasks — Target Dates — Objectives — Costs and Metrics — Summary and Forecast

Costs and Metrics:

	Expended / Completed	Budgeted / Required
Expenses	135	150
Work Instructions	580	580
Records	307	307

Expended / Budgeted; Completed / Required; = G; = Y

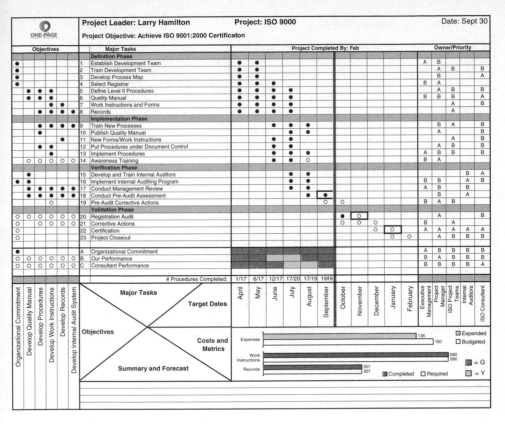

FIGURE 5.18 *The OPPM in Our ISO Registration OPPM/A3*

 To customize this document, download it to your hard drive from the following web site: www.oppmi.com. The document can be opened, edited, and printed using Microsoft Excel or another popular spreadsheet application.

back to the beginning and realize that in the beginning we doubted we could even meet the target date.

Figure 5.18 presents our OPPM for the ISO registration effort.

CHECK

A very important step of the PDCA cycle occurs both as the implementation of the improvement is rolled out and subsequent to the implementation. This step is often overlooked but must not be. Check the affects and results of the improvement both as the improvement is implemented and in the future, after the improvement effort.

This is not a simple check to see that everything is done. It is a careful review of the result(s) or progress in light of the target(s) or schedule. It is also an effort to gain an understanding of what has been learned from this effort. It is a time of reflection. It is particularly important that we ask how we could have done better and how we would better approach this problem or effort in the future. It is an effort to learn as much as we possibly can from this experience. As we check the improvement, we can gain a greater understanding of the improvement, its effects, and the direction of future improvements.

What did we learn from our ISO registration effort? First, contrary to the traditional thought of many consultants, we began with the hypothesis that we could achieve ISO registration for far less than the $500,000 price tags that we were being told to expect, and that we could complete the registration process in far less time than the two years that we were being told it would take. We confirmed our hypothesis that we could do so by achieving ISO registration for less than $200,000 and in less than six months.

Second, our ISO registration effort reinforced the importance and value of a very good project manager who owns the project. Larry Hamilton was our project manager and he worked tirelessly and fearlessly to ensure that every effort was being made to meet our objectives. It is a mistake to think that a consultant would assume this level of ownership. It simply can't be.

Both the heart and mind are required in any great effort to improve—not just the mind.

Third, we could have achieved ISO registration even earlier in the history of our company had we attempted to do so. In other words, we should not have postponed this effort as we did.

Fourth, strong goals (e.g., achieving ISO registration in less than six months) can bring out in some people capabilities which we have not previously seen in those people. It may even be a level of performance that exceeds their own personal belief. Deb Hohenthal had worked for our company for many years in a number of different capacities. Many of her assignments focused on her very gifted ability to write. So, we took advantage of this writing skill in drafting our quality manual. The pressures of this initiative were such, however, that all team members were being asked to do more and to step out of their previous comfort zones.

We needed not only a good quality manual but also someone to train others in the content and use of the manual. It seemed best to ask Deb to do this because she was most familiar with the content. It also seemed natural that she could best help us with our self-audits. Deb not only succeeded in the assignments we gave her, she emerged as our ISO leader, and to this day she continues to lead our ISO efforts.

Fifth, we had seen ISO and Lean as not complementary of one another. By carefully integrating ISO into our Tanner Improvement System, we learned that ISO could be complementary to Lean. We did just as the great leaders of Toyota had done. We took the best that we could find in the ISO thinking and integrated it into our own great Tanner Improvement System. In the end we were and are to this day a better and stronger company. This learning strengthened our will and our belief that to be a great company one must listen well, consider carefully, maintain an open mind, and always be willing to change.

Sixth, we once again confirmed that even a complex project can be simplified. It is a balance between efficient and sufficient. The check phase of our ISO is presented in Figure 5.19.

ACT

The step of Check is followed immediately by an action or actions —ACT. The action can range from a simple tweaking of the improvement or some additional training to abandonment of the improvement due to certain unforeseen problems or a failure to prove the desired results. In many instances, the action will be the definition, planning, and scheduling of the next improvement effort, the next PDCA cycle.

It is most important that the Act step not be overlooked, for it is in this step that:

- Learning is captured and applied
- The cycle of continuous improvement is ensured

We knew as we completed our ISO registration effort that achieving ISO registration was simply a milestone passed.

Check

From the beginning of our efforts to achieve ISO registration there have been many and sometimes difficult challenges. As we have reviewed our progress and the completion of this effort, the following take-aways have risen to the top and need to be passed on to future efforts.

1. Its is always possible to reduce time and cost without sacrificing quality. With teamwork, leadership, strong goals and our hearts and minds we reduced the expected cost of the project from approx. $500k to less than $200k. We reduced the time from an expected 2 year period to less than 6 months.

2. A good, strong project manager is a critical element of success. The mind of a consultant is important. The heart *and* mind of one of our own, a good project manager, are far more important.

3. We should not have delayed our pursuit of ISO. We must always push forward, past our concerns and our fears. WE can do more than we think we can. The power is in WE.

4. Strong goals and good leadership develop our people and their capabilities.

5. Remember always to keep an open mind, to listen carefully, to always be willing to change. Our processes can always be improved as we have learned as we have integrated the best of ISO into our own great TIS system.

6. Once again we have seen that the complex can be made simple by removing the waste and focusing on the value added. It is balance between efficient and sufficient.

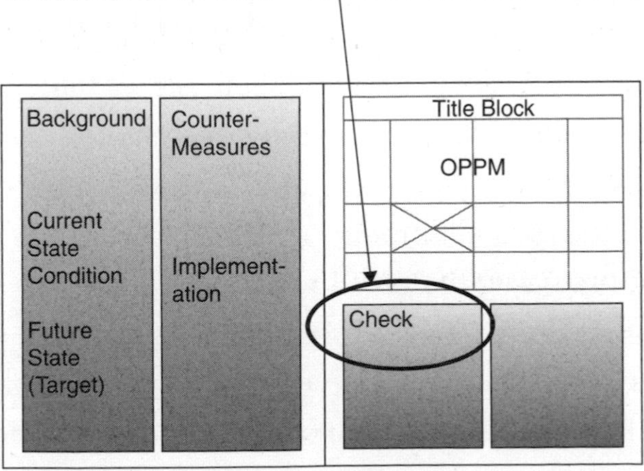

FIGURE 5.19 *OPPM/A3 ISO Registration Check Statement*

It was clear that our efforts would need to continue on for some time until the changes relative to ISO would become ingrained in our way of being. Therefore, one of the first actions planned was a series of trainings and self-audits.

Our Canadian operation would also need to become ISO registered. As we began discussing how best to approach the ISO registration of our Canadian operation, we reviewed the events of our ISO registration experience and determined, contrary to the thoughts of our ISO consultant, that we could achieve this without the use of a consultant. We sent our project manager, Larry Hamilton, to Canada and were successful in that ISO registration both in record time and without an ISO consultant.

There were other actions planned at this time as well, all of which were built upon what we had learned from our ISO registration initiative. One well-executed PDCA cycle very often perpetuates another. This is real continuous improvement. The Act phase of our ISO effort is presented in Figure 5.20.

Our OPPM/A3 ISO registration effort is just one of many of our applications of the OPPM/A3. Without exception, the use of the OPPM/A3 has enhanced the success of every project to which it has been applied. Ambiguities have been replaced with clear understanding and focused alignment of efforts. Objectives have been more easily realized in less time and often with less expenditure. Most importantly, the engagement of our people and their creative energies has increased. All of this has led to greater successes and accelerated company growth.

Act

Our effort towards completion of ISO registration reinforced several of our principles and beliefs. To help ingrain these thoughts into our culture, we are scheduling the inclusion of several of our ISO registration experiences in four of our upcoming company newsletters. We are encouraging the telling of this story in company meetings. We have scheduled time with our trainers and team leaders to review the experience with them and to encourage them to use the story as they teach and train our people.

Two weeks from now our team will meet and discuss how the OPPM/A3 was used during this initiative. We have a list of suggested improvements, and these will be reviewed and implemented where appropriate.

We have initiated and or developing our planning OPPM/A3 for our Canadian ISO registration.

We will develop four enhanced and focused ISO training classes to be scheduled over the next year. We are recommending that every employee attend all four sessions during the next year.

To further ingrain changes related to ISO, we will be conducting an ISO self-audit at the end of each quarter of 2004.

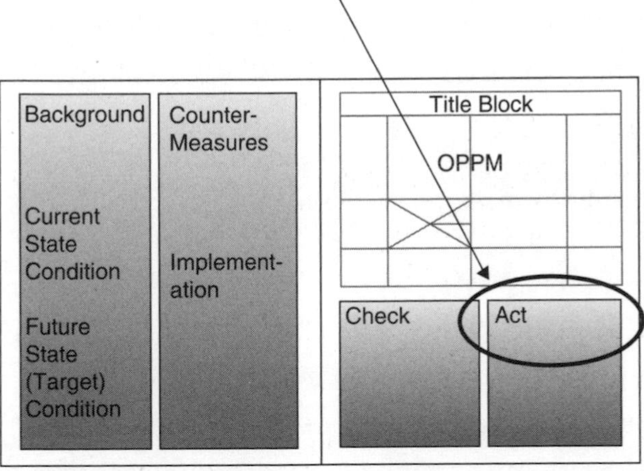

FIGURE 5.20 *OPPM/A3 ISO Registration Act Statement*

CHAPTER

The Project Management Office and Execution

Two elements of execution, as defined by Larry Bossidy and Ram Charan in their book, *Execution—The Discipline of Getting Things Done*, include:

- A discipline of meshing strategy with reality, aligning people with goals, and achieving the results promised.

And

- The way to link the three core processes of any business—the people process, the strategy process, and the operating plan—together to get things done on-time.

We have found in our teaching, consulting, and personal management experience that a powerful and effective project management office (PMO) provides the necessary champion and cohesive catalyst required to mesh and link.

Every project is run from some place. A small project could be run from someone's desk and might be one of several responsibilities of that person. Or, a project could be coordinated from a central office devoted exclusively to corporate project communication. Or a very large project could have its own office.

The Project Management Office, or PMO, is the person or group of people who have at least eight high-level, company-wide project responsibilities, all focused on seeing that projects are set up and managed for success.

This chapter is about how the PMO can use the OPPM effectively to address each of these eight project responsibilities.

1. PROJECT DASHBOARD

The first responsibility of the PMO is to maintain the dashboard for the organization's projects. The PMO tracks, at a high level, the progress of projects and reports them to upper management. This is a vital responsibility of the PMO. It reports to the company's executives in a way that allows them to know what is going on with projects and when attention is needed. The PMO keeps senior management fully aware, at a high level, of these basic areas:

- *The owners:* who are those responsible for various parts of a project
- *The cost:* how much the project has and will cost, and whether it is currently on-budget or off-budget and by how much
- *The tasks:* how the deliverables and activities of the project are progressing versus the plan
- *The time line:* when various project tasks are finished or are expected to be completed
- *The objectives:* the what (what the project is) and the why (why it is being done)

The PMO communicates these aspects of projects to executives for as long as the projects are under development or being completed. The role of the OPPM in the PMO is to be a tool that efficiently communicates essential information from the PMO to senior management. We don't think it is an overstatement to say the OPPM is *essential* to an effective PMO. It is essential because it consolidates all important information in one place. It is a critical communication link between a company's projects and its senior leaders. Think of it as the means by which information flows into and out of a PMO. And it manages that information by putting it into a form that's easily created, read, and understood. Without the OPPM, the PMO will be inundated with too much information. Moreover, their reporting output will be crisp and consolidated into a single OPPM. It is the *dashboard.*

The OPPM makes possible the PMO's ability to collect, analyze, and report a massive amount of project information. It facilitates the operational efficiency and the communication effectiveness of the PMO. By requiring every manager to report with the OPPM, you only get one page from each. It's a winnowing and summarization, as well as the underpinning standard of excellence for a PMO.

2. CORPORATE PROJECT METHODOLOGY

The second important responsibility of the PMO is to be the keeper of the flame, the czar of the company's corporate project methodology. It must also provide tools to support that methodology. Further, the PMO is responsible for project management systems. The value of the OPPM is, in effect, the communication system. The PMO uses the OPPM as the methodology for reporting and communicating about projects. The PMO ensures that every project manager knows how to use the OPPM. Without going too far in making claims for the tool, the OPPM helps promote professionalism in project management within an organization. It provides a protocol from which the discipline of project management can be reinforced.

3. PROJECT TRAINING

Third, the PMO has the responsibility to train and mentor project managers as they develop their skills. For example, our goal at O.C. Tanner is to have at least 95 percent of our people trained on and using the OPPM at any given time. The process for doing this: Our project managers and those who work on projects read *The One-Page Project Manager* and receive general and specific training about the tool from project managers who have worked with the tool, and generally get encouragement from the PMO to use the tool. Of course, it helps that they experience the tool firsthand and discuss its use over time. This allows users to become more familiar and comfortable with it.

In addition to training on the OPPM, other reading materials, lectures, and seminars are encouraged to drive an expanding working knowledge of all aspects of project management's "body of knowledge."

4. CONSISTENT APPLICATION

The PMO ensures the consistent application of the methodology. This takes energy because people want to depart from the standard the organization establishes. Users think they have ways to improve the OPPM or that their project is so special it needs its own version of the OPPM. The PMO needs to manage such tendencies. It's not that the OPPM cannot be improved or should not be modified for specific situations, but such changes must be done at a high level to prevent balkanization of the tool. If left unchecked, such tendencies will lead, in short order, to many different OPPM formats, thereby losing the power of standardization and consistency.

The PMO must balance a standard methodology against continuous improvement. There is real value in consistency. It helps reinforce in the minds of users the value of the tool. It keeps project managers and team members focused on what is important. It makes it easier for everyone in the organization to learn how to create, use, and interpret the tool. Just the right balance between consistency and creativity yields efficiency and excellence.

And it helps management understand what the tool is communicating. Imagine an organization with many projects, each with its fundamentally different OPPM. Senior management will have to decipher what each version of the OPPM is trying to communicate, which negates much of the benefit of having a simple and consistent tool used across an organization, with relatively minor variations for different types of projects. The bottom line: **The OPPM is the PMO's single most important communication tool.**

Keep in mind that for large projects the OPPM does not eliminate, replace, or substitute for any tool your project managers want to use, such as Microsoft Project or Oracle's Primavera software. It is in addition to the tools you are already using. A major project may have an OPPM at the top and then, drilling down, additional OPPMs for various aspects of the project. With a software project, we might use one OPPM for the hiring of a consultant, another for choosing the software, another for the limited rollout and testing of the software, and so on. At the top is an OPPM that reports on all those under it. It is this top-most OPPM that senior management sees.

The head of projects needs to strike a balance between standardization and customization. What this executive must be on guard for is the tendency of the user to customize the OPPM to the point where it is dramatically different from one project to another, or from one department to another. Certain things *must* remain the same, such as the colors used (and their meanings) and the use of empty circles to convey an aspect of a project not yet completed, and a filled-in circle that signifies completion. These aspects of the OPPM don't change.

However, some aspects of the tool can be changed. For example, some projects may use time periods of one week each, whereas others use monthly periods. Some OPPMs may incorporate graphs or charts, whereas others will not. It's the job of the head of the PMO to exercise the judgment necessary to maintain standards while allowing creativity, individual ownership, and innovation.

It's important to understand that the PMO produces a consolidated OPPM that is a summary of all the projects the office is tracking. The project managers for each project submit their OPPMs to the PMO, where they are, in turn, summarized onto a consolidated OPPM, which is essentially an OPPM that lists all current and recently completed projects. In this way, senior management can quickly see the status of all the projects happening in the organization. If they want more information about individual projects, they can read the OPPMs for those projects, often precluding inefficient inquiry with the project team.

5. PROJECT PUBLIC RELATIONS

We've talked a lot about how the OPPM communicates *up* an organization to senior management, but it also is able to communicate to those within or outside the organization who might have a tangential interest in the particular project. The PMO can use the tool to market and communicate aspects of a project *out* to audiences who might have a need to know about the project but are not intimately involved with it. Its simplicity makes it a great tool for such communication. Examples of outward audiences to whom the OPPM communicates include: suppliers, other managers within the company, the company's human resources department (which wants to keep track of who is working on what projects), the internal audit department, and the sales department (which wants a quick look at how things are progressing on new products so it knows when new products will become available).

By the way, the OPPM has an additional benefit that might not be immediately obvious—namely, that it can shorten management meetings. Because everyone is reading from the same page, both literally and metaphorically, when the PMO holds meetings, participants can quickly get up to speed about the essential aspects of the project. This is a real time-saver. So many management meetings are too long. With the OPPM, you can reference back to the tool because everyone knows and understands it. Attention is keen when issues are germane to a person's area of responsibility. When other issues are perused, interest may dissipate. The OPPM helps make discussions clear, concise, and to the point, which is key to keeping everyone engaged.

6. PROJECT PRIORITIZATION

The OPPM helps the PMO prioritize its portfolio of projects. When the PMO compiles an OPPM that includes all projects, those that make it onto the tool automatically get priority. They get funded. They get resources ahead of other projects.

The OPPM also makes clear the demands that various projects are making on an organization. When a project appears on the corporate OPPM and the reader sees that the project involves 303 people, or however many, it reminds everyone of the burden of certain projects and the load these projects are placing on various departments and the organization as a whole. The tool allows management to see the money and people being devoted to various projects and the need to balance the use of those and other resources with the day-to-day activities of the business. It's often difficult to keep projects and the daily demands of running a business in proper perspective. Projects are undertaken to make tomorrow's customer orders better, but this may come at the expense of today's orders. The OPPM, because it paints such a clear, readily accessible picture of projects, helps management keep a balance between now and the future.

7. PROJECT REVIEW AND CORRECTIVE ACTION

The consolidated OPPM facilitates the PMO's and senior management's attention to needed corrective action. The PMO conducts project reviews prior to reporting on those projects. The OPPM causes the PMO and the project team to think about the important aspects of a project. Sure, teams will think about time lines and budgets regardless of whether they use the OPPM, but they don't often think about who the owners are for each part of a project or how various parts of a project relate to important objectives or strategic goals. The OPPM makes these important connections readily apparent.

By using the OPPM, you and your team will have to think about all the essential elements of a project, as well as relationships between parts of the project, plus the people involved with it. And because the OPPM saves time, you will have the time to do this type of thorough planning. The work of the PMO ends up being more complete and effective because of the OPPM.

One more thing: Because the OPPM ties performance to individuals (the owners), when things go well, senior management can see it on the OPPM and take action, such as giving a compliment or otherwise providing positive recognition. The tool helps to energize a whole culture of recognition, not just corrective action.

8. PROJECT ARCHIVES AND CONTINUOUS IMPROVEMENT

By holding onto the OPPMs for each project (which is easy to do because even a large project probably has an OPPM generated once a week (which is 52 pages for a one-year project), the PMO is able to easily create and maintain an archive of completed projects.

These OPPMs become a repository of project learning. As George Santayana famously said, "Those who cannot learn from history are doomed to repeat it." Such an archive is a means by which future project leaders and teams can learn. It shows how things were done, how projects progressed, where challenges occurred, and how they were overcome. Using the OPPM to create a history is easy and efficient. And when a project is completed, the PMO just needs to have all the OPPMs bound and placed in a file cabinet, with electronic copies easily stored and retrieved.

Example

The PMO provides a monthly report to management which contains the current OPPM for each strategic project. A summary OPPM showing the performance of all projects serves as the cover page. This summary OPPM for the PMO must communicate for each corporate project:

- Alignment with company strategy
- Correlation to the annual operating plan
- Capital budget tracking
- Expense budget tracking
- People involved
- Current performance or status
- On-time versus lateness
- Assigned project manager
- Executive team responsibilities
- A consolidation and summation

This is the heart of the communication network.

Figure 6.1 is a general template. Figure 6.2 is an example from the fictitious Mount Olympus Company. You

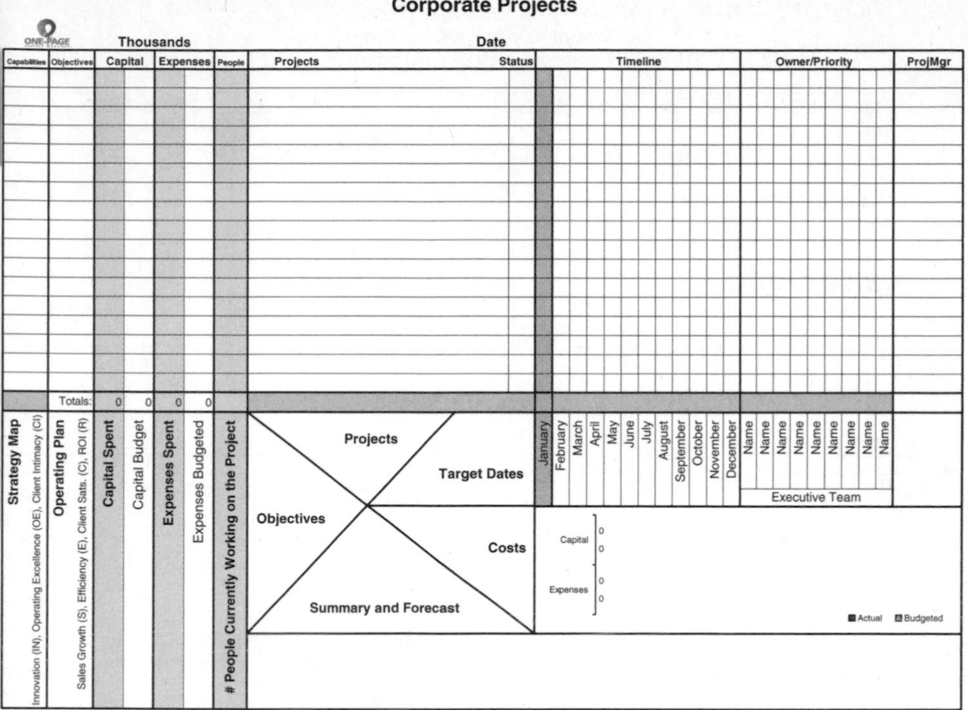

Corporate Projects
ONE-PAGE
Thousands
Date
Capabilities
Objectives
Capital
Expenses
People
Projects
Status
Timeline
Owner/Priority
ProjMgr
Totals:
0 0 0 0
Strategy Map
Innovation (IN), Operating Excellence (OE), Client Intimacy (CI)
Operating Plan
Sales Growth (S), Efficiency (E), Client Sats. (C), ROI (R)
Capital Spent
Capital Budget
Expenses Spent
Expenses Budgeted
People Currently Working on the Project
Projects
Target Dates
Objectives
Costs
Summary and Forecast
January
February
March
April
May
June
July
August
September
October
November
December
Name
Executive Team
Capital
Expenses
Actual
Budgeted

FIGURE 6.1 *Project Office Template*

Copyright O.C. Tanner 2009. To customize this document, download it to your hard drive from the following web site: www.oppmi.com. The document can be opened, edited, and printed using Microsoft Excel or another popular spreadsheet application.

will see another example of this in the next chapter. Let's jump right into reading the November year-to-date report.

If you look at the fourth heading from the left, you will see Expenses. And at the bottom of the two columns under Expenses are the labels Expenses Spent and Expenses Budgeted. The first reports what has actually been spent, while the second reports on the amount budgeted, or what was expected to be spent. The fifth line down in Figure 6.2, for example, relates to the Zeta project. It is budgeted at $350,000, but only $220,000 has

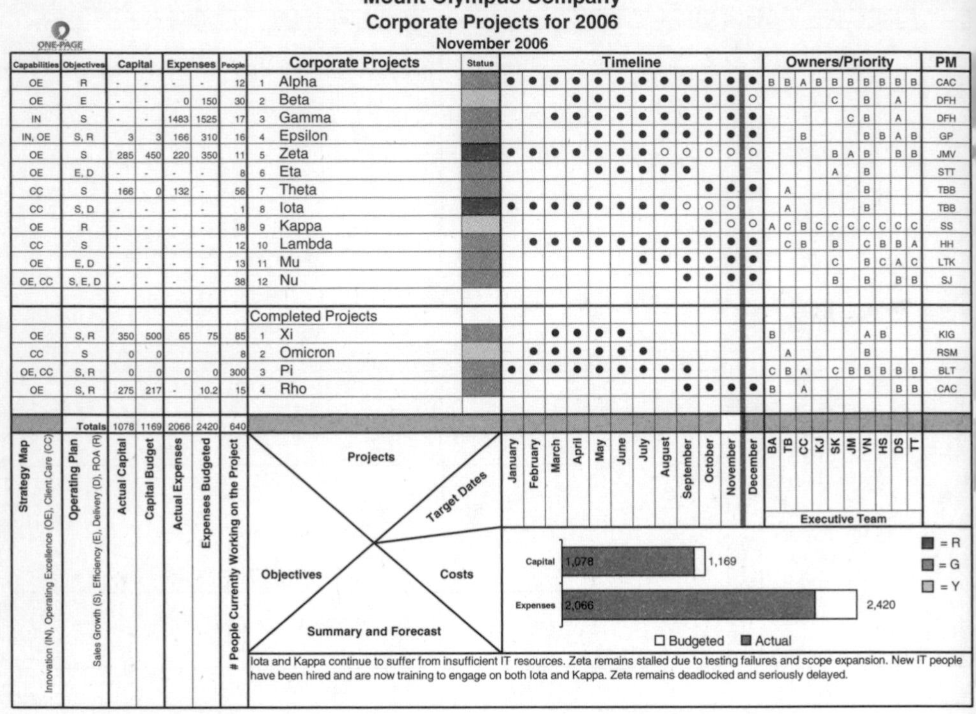

FIGURE 6.2 *Mount Olympus Company Project Office Report*

been spent, so it is $130,000, under budget. Note, however, that the project is behind schedule.

In fact, if you look under Timeline. you will see the heavy vertical line, which tells you the month of this OPPM is November. Yet, this particular project has four empty dots to the left of this line, indicating the project is four months behind schedule. In fact, three projects are behind schedule, which is indicated by the number of projects whose dots are not filled in all the way to the current time. Eight of the projects are ahead of schedule (which is indicated by filled-in dots to the right of the heavy vertical line).

A project such as the Epsilon, the fourth project from the top, does not have any dots until May, which is when the project started. The sixth project down, Eta, has dots that stop in September, indicating when the project was projected to end. With these timeline dots, you can tell when projects begin and end (or started or continue beyond the scope of this OPPM) and which projects are on-time, behind, or ahead of schedule.

The first column on the left is labeled Capabilities. At the bottom of that column are listed the three strategic goals of the company: Innovation, Operating Excellence, and Client Care. Mount Olympus is committed to being an innovator (IN) in its market, excellent in how it conducts its operations (OE), and superior in how it takes care of its clients (CC). If a project does not address a strategic goal the box will be conspicuously blank. You can see how each project connects to strategic goals in this column. The Zeta project has OE in this column, which lets the reader know that this project is tied into the company's strategic goal of being an excellent operating organization.

The second column to the right addresses operating goals. These include Sales Growth (S), Efficiency (E), Delivery (D), and Return On Assets (R), and are short-term rather than strategic. These are self-evident except perhaps for on-time delivery, which is one metric that reflects client satisfaction. The operating purpose of the Zeta project is to spur sales, so this project is tied to the operating goal of sales growth.

To the left of Expenses is Capital, which refers to a project's capital expenses. Capital expenses typically relate to the purchase of tangible items such as equipment that have useful lives of more than one year. This is what shows up on the balance sheet, whereas expenses show up on the income statement. With the Zeta project, the capital budget is $450,000, of which $285,000 has been invested.

The column to the right of this, labeled People, lists the number of employees involved with each project. This lets management know the number of people committed to any given project at any given time. The Zeta project involves 11 people (this includes both full- and part-time employees, and not full-time equivalents [FTEs]). We're just counting noses, people who are spending some of their time on the project. Experience has shown that attempting to be more granular with the people number is ineffective. Actual hours spent is important, but they are not critical at this level.

The last column on the right, PM, refers to project manager. The PM for the Zeta project we've been looking at is John, who is responsible for this project. Just to the left of this is a heading reading Owners/Property. These are the senior managers under whose department the project is being done. Folks running the projects and have ownership of them are listed by their priority of importance (A owners own the project with principal responsibility, whereas B and C owners are helpers with decreasing responsibility).

The status column in the middle of the page (which will print in color) indicates the general performance of each project. If green, the project is going well—its time line and budget are basically where they should be. There is no cause for concern. Yellow indicates there are some issues, but there is still time to recover; these are not projects senior management needs to be worried about at the present time. The project may be a bit behind schedule, a bit over budget, or have some other concern, but in the end, the project should be completed in an acceptable fashion without much intervention from senior management. The red rectangles are projects in trouble. The status of both the Zeta and the Iota projects are shown in red. The Zeta project, as noted, is four months behind schedule. Such projects often require intervention from senior management who can secure cross-department assistance or reset priorities.

The rectangle near the lower right-hand corner of the consolidated OPPM shows the consolidated capital and expense budgets. The Capital budget totals $1,169,000, of which $1,078,000 has been spent. The Expense budget totals $2,420,000, of which $2,066,000 has been spent. These are green, indicating there is, overall, no cause for concern relating to the budgets.

The four projects listed below the heavy horizontal line near the middle of the page—Xi, Omicron, Pi, and Rho—are recent projects that have been completed. You can tell they are finished because all circles are filled in, and they have no circles in the timeline.

In the rectangle at the bottom of the page is the Summary and Forecast. It mentions that projects Iota and Kappa continue to suffer from insufficient

IT resources. Zeta remains stalled due to testing failures and scope expansion. New IT people have been deployed on Iota and Kappa. Zeta remains deadlocked and seriously delayed. You want to succinctly answer the questions posed by delays in the schedules and the reds and yellows. After your explanations, give a high level forecast of future expectations.

With this consolidated OPPM from the PMO, senior management can quickly see how all projects are progressing, how they're linked to strategies, and who owns them. All of this can be gleaned by the CEO and others with a quick read of this tool. Providing so much detail in easily digestible form helps the PMO fulfill its objective to communicate the progress of the company's projects. It helps the PMO achieve the eight prime objectives mentioned at the start of this chapter.

1. A Project Dashboard
2. A Corporate Project Methodology
3. Project Training
4. Consistent Application of the Methodology
5. Project Public Relations
6. Project Prioritizations
7. Project Review and Corrective Action
8. Project Archives and Continuous Improvement

As you can now see, the OPPM is essential to an effective PMO.

CHAPTER

OPPMs, A3s, and Strategy Deployment

Typically, during strategic planning time, executives sequester themselves in a retreat-like setting armed with sales and market projections and some semblance of customer input. The output of this event is a nice, bound presentation that sits on the shelf and collects dust until the next planning session begins. At that time, the executives take it off the shelf and refresh their memory as to the grandiose plan of yesteryear, wondering how they ever got so far off course. . . .

A major contributor to this problem is the typical strategic planning process. Many companies fail to properly execute using information systems intended for planning and then fail to properly execute a plan driven by data gathered from those same information systems. The fault lies not in the information systems, rather in the planning process and in the execution process.

Matt Lanius

http://www.isixsigma.com/library/content/c060605a.asp

This chapter is about getting past the failure of most strategic planning efforts and the malaise of taking time to do strategic planning. We tell you how to use the OPPM/A3 to execute your strategic planning efforts and how this effort is simplified through the use of the OPPM/A3.

In this chapter, the reader will learn about:

- The Lean practice of strategy deployment, sometimes called policy deployment
- The meaning of *hoshin kanri*
- The use of the OPPM/A3 in strategy deployment
- Most importantly, how to execute strategic planning

WHAT IS STRATEGY DEPLOYMENT?

Strategy deployment is a critical element of a Lean management system. In "Lean speak" strategy deployment is often referred to as *hoshin kanri*, the Japanese wording for strategy deployment or, more correctly, policy deployment. Strategy deployment via the OPPM/A3 is a very refined and yet simple practice for the execution of business strategy. The A3 and OPPM are the primary tools of strategy deployment and greatly facilitate this practice.

In Lean or Toyota verbiage, a very basic OPPM is known as an x-matrix. The Lean practitioner will note, however, that the OPPM is not just a simple x-matrix, but more like an x-matrix on steroids.

The purpose of strategy deployment is to provide *a plan or course of action that will guide the day-to-day decisions and management of the business to a most expeditious execution of the business strategy.* It is notably different from what many of us have experienced with strategic planning efforts.

Deployment refers to the *systematic allocation of resources*. Deployment is the planning of which resources are best used in the execution of the plan as well as a definition of when, where, and how these resources will be used.

The A3 is a statement of the strategy, the determination of the strategy, its objective(s), and its success. The OPPM is a statement of the deployment and usage of resources needed to accomplish the strategy. Together, the A3 and the OPPM state in a single document everything critical about a strategic deployment.

THE STRATEGY DEPLOYMENT PRACTICE

The practice of strategy deployment is:

- A downward cascading system of planning
- An upward aggregation of reporting

Through the planning cascade and the reporting aggregation, all levels of the organization are involved and aligned to the strategic objectives of the organization, and potentially all personnel are involved in developing the results and outcome of the strategy. Each level of planning supports in ever greater detail the plan above it, its parent plan. A graphical depiction is presented in Figure 7.1. The highest-level plan is a broad statement of the strategic efforts to be made, providing vision, direction, targets, and objectives. The lowest-level plans are very detailed statements of specific actions and objectives to be accomplished within defined time periods.

The processes of the human body are analogous to the process of strategy deployment. The mind does not control every action of the body. The mind, for example, will send a signal to the heart that more pumping is needed, but the activities of the heart are then autonomous. Additionally, the heart does not tell the cells in the heart specifically what to do. Instead, as the cells receive inputs from their immediate environment, they respond appropriately. How they then respond affects the output of the heart, and how the heart responds affects the body.

Strategy deployment is similar in that the entirety of the strategic plan and the execution of the strategic plan are not determined by the heads of the organization, but rather through the autonomous actions of interdependent groups within the organization. In this chapter, we will present three levels of strategy deployment: corporate, business function, and team. These three levels are analogous to mind, organ, and cell. The mind does not dictate in detail the actions taken at the cell level.

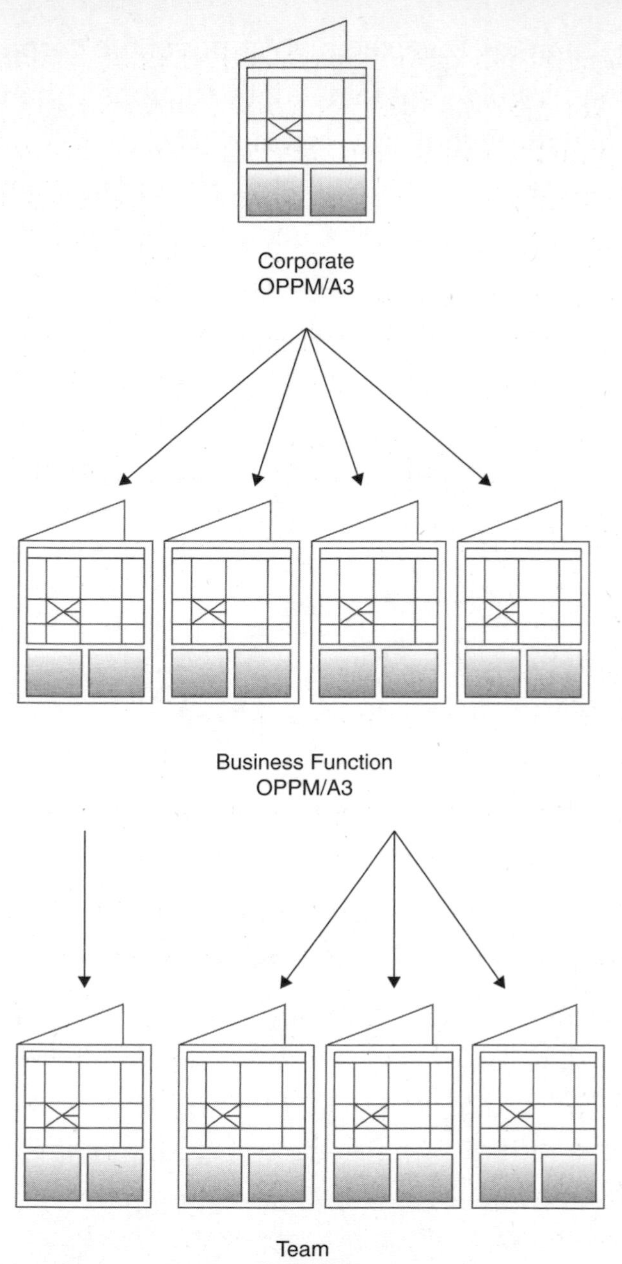

FIGURE 7.1 *A Graphical Depiction of a Strategy Deployment Cascade*

In a like manner, the executive group at the corporate level does not plan out in detail the actions and initiatives taken throughout the organization.

Each strategy deployment level, rather autonomously, manages its own Plan, Do, Check, and Act activities. Each level does this in context of and in support of the environment in which it is placed by the parent level. The OPPM/A3 is the best tool for facilitating the PDCA at each level.

A few common characteristics of strategy deployment plans are:

- Strategy deployment and each level of planning are built on cycles of PDCA
- Each plan is presented as an OPPM/A3 or, in Japanese, a *hoshin*
- Each OPPM/A3 serves both as a plan and a report of accomplishment
- Each plan supports the strategy and goals of the plan above it with appropriate tasks and actions
- For small- and many medium-size businesses, three levels of planning are generally sufficient. Larger companies, with many geographically dispersed divisions or multiple industries may require additional levels of strategy deployment planning.

PDCA is typically a never-ending series of PDCA cycles. The completion of one cycle of PDCA generates the next cycle of PDCA. Often these cycles are nested one within another. Before the first cycle can begin, a review of business conditions and the business environment is conducted. Strategy deployment begins with a review of business conditions and environment. Thomas L. Jackson, in his text, *Hoshin Kanri for the Lean Enterprise*, uses the word *scan* in lieu of the word *review* for this phase preceding to PDCA and strategy deployment.

Corporate OPPM/A3

Strategy deployment is initiated by the executive leadership of the organization. They are responsible for the review (scan) of the business and its environment. The executive leadership will call on others throughout the organization and from outside the organization to assist them in their review. When they are satisfied that they have a good view of the state of the organization and its environment, they then formulate the strategy of the organization for the next three to five years. This is captured in an OPPM/A3.

Many organizations are prone to identifying every strategic need that they can possibly see. It is very important that they reduce the set of strategic needs to only those strategic issues that are of most importance to the success of the organization. It may help to think of the reduced set of strategies as being only those that are truly breakthrough objectives. Planning too many strategic directions diffuses the efforts of the organization and weakens its ability to move forward strategically. It is strongly suggested that an organization not pursue more than three to five truly breakthrough objectives in any strategy deployment period.

Each breakthrough objective with its plan is often presented in a separate OPPM/A3. Some organizations state their strategies on a single A3 and OPPM, but this practice can sometimes make the A3 and the OPPM a bit messy and difficult to read.

The executive group must then define the set of initiatives and tactics that will bring to fruition each desired strategy (breakthrough objective). In today's rapidly changing environment it is very difficult if not impossible to see clearly the strategic steps and actions that need to be taken over a three-to-five-year period. A long view is necessary to maintain a definitive strategic direction, but we have found that people begin to lose their focus and drive when executing plans and projects that last more than about four months. The best practice then is to create in addition to the three-to-five-year strategic objectives a detailed plan (OPPM/A3) of shorter term initiatives that are not more than about one year in length. At the end of that period, celebrate the accomplishments and develop the next period plan using the better view of the future available at that point in time as well as the learning from the previous period. This is the PDCA cycle. Plan. Execute the plan. Check the results. Act on the results, and pass the learning to the next PDCA cycle.

Whereas the determination of the three-to-five-year key strategies is mostly the work of executive leadership, the determination required to support one-year initiatives and tactics is a collaborative effort involving management from outside the executive leadership group and other special knowledge individuals in the organization. The collaborative effort occurs in a catchball fashion.

CATCHBALL

Catchball refers to the baseball practice of throwing a ball back and forth. In a good catchball session, each thrower will test the other with throws of varying angles and velocities. The two throwers talk with one another and often give feedback on each throw and catch. Over time, both throwers improve their ability to catch and throw the baseball.

Catchball in strategy deployment is the practice of throwing the plans back and forth between each planning level. The first throw of the plan from executive management to operating leaders or management asks, in effect, Can you do this plan? Does it make sense? What changes should we make to improve the plan?

The operating leaders then throw the plan back to the executive leadership, perhaps with a slightly different curve to the plan. The curve may be: Did you consider . . . ? The plan requires a resource that is not yet available. We could more effectively meet the desired objective by. . . .

This communicating of the plans between each level continues until each plan level is satisfied with the plan and comfortable that the plans represent the best that can be done in the next period of time.

The work of the executive group and those who work with them can be captured in the first OPPM and A3.

This first or highest-level OPPM captures on a single page the:

- Strategies/breakthrough objectives
- Initiatives
- Actions/tactics
- Schedules
- Budgets
- The leaders of each action/tactic

The A3 then captures:

- Key information from the review that is relevant to the selected key strategies
- Other strategies that were considered but not selected as breakthrough objectives
- The reasoning behind the strategy selections
- Reasoning behind the initiatives, goals and targets
- The vision of the strategies—that which will be achieved by the breakthrough objectives
- The desired business impact

The A3 is in effect a statement of the analysis, the hypothesis, the experiment at hand, and, as the strategic period advances, a statement of proven results. This is the scientific method in practice. The reader should note the cycles of PDCA in both the OPPM and the A3. We include the OPPM in the A3 and thereby capture on a single sheet of paper and in a most succinct manner all of the most important information relative to the strategy and its plan.

Corporate OPPM/A3

We call the document summarizing the first level of strategy deployment a corporate OPPM/A3 to differentiate it from other strategy deployment levels throughout this book. An example of the corporate OPPM included in the corporate OPPM/A3 is given in Figure 7.2.

The OPPM is read in a clockwise manner, one quarter at a time, beginning with the left-hand side of page. At the bottom left-hand side of the page are stated the three to five strategies or breakthrough objectives. In this example we have shown only two strategies to provide a simpler example.

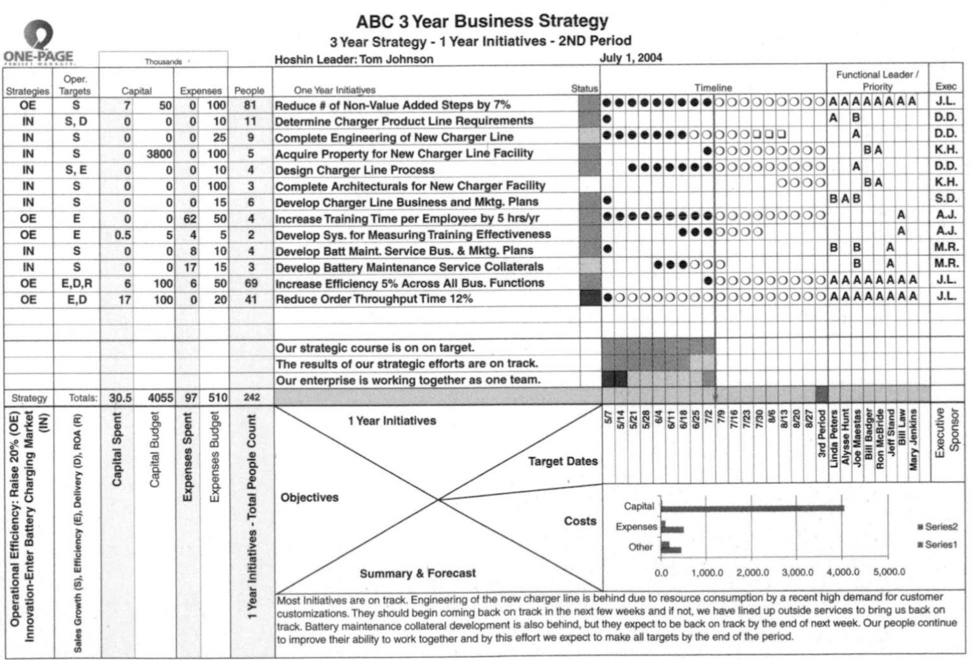

ABC 3 Year Business Strategy

3 Year Strategy - 1 Year Initiatives - 2ND Period

Hoshin Leader: Tom Johnson — July 1, 2004

ONE-PAGE

Strategies	Oper. Targets	Capital (Thousands)		Expenses (Thousands)		People	One Year Initiatives	Timeline	Linda Peters	Alysse Hunt	Joe Maestas	Bill Badger	Ron McBride	Jeff Stand	Bill Law	Mary Jenkins	Exec
OE	S	7	50	0	100	81	Reduce # of Non-Value Added Steps by 7%	●●●●●●●●●○○○○○○○○○	A	A	A	A	A	A	A	A	J.L.
IN	S, D	0	0	0	10	11	Determine Charger Product Line Requirements	●	A		B						D.D.
IN	S	0	0	0	25	9	Complete Engineering of New Charger Line	●●●●●●●○○○○○❑❑❑			A						D.D.
IN	S	0	3800	0	100	5	Acquire Property for New Charger Line Facility	●○○○○○○○○○				B	A				K.H.
IN	S, E	0	0	0	10	4	Design Charger Line Process	●●●●●●●○○○○○○○○○			A						D.D.
IN	S	0	0	0	100	3	Complete Architecturals for New Charger Facility	○○○○				B	A				K.H.
IN	S	0	0	0	15	6	Develop Charger Line Business and Mktg. Plans	●	B	A	B						S.D.
OE	E	0	0	62	50	4	Increase Training Time per Employee by 5 hrs/yr	●●●●●●●●●○○○○○○○○○							A		A.J.
OE	E	0.5	5	4	5	2	Develop Sys. for Measuring Training Effectiveness	●●●○○○○							A		A.J.
IN	S	0	0	8	10	4	Develop Batt Maint. Service Bus. & Mktg. Plans	●	B		B			A			M.R.
IN	S	0	0	17	15	3	Develop Battery Maintenance Service Collaterals	●●●○○○			B			A			M.R.
OE	E,D,R	6	100	6	50	69	Increase Efficiency 5% Across All Bus. Functions	●○○○○○○○○○	A	A	A	A	A	A	A	A	J.L.
OE	E,D	17	100	0	20	41	Reduce Order Throughput Time 12%	●○○○○○○○○○○○○○○○○○	A	A	A	A	A	A	A	A	J.L.
							Our strategic course is on on target.										
							The results of our strategic efforts are on track.										
							Our enterprise is working together as one team.										
Strategy	Totals:	30.5	4055	97	510	242											

Most Initiatives are on track. Engineering of the new charger line is behind due to resource consumption by a recent high demand for customer customizations. They should begin coming back on track in the next few weeks and if not, we have lined up outside services to bring us back on track. Battery maintenance collateral development is also behind, but they expect to be back on track by the end of next week. Our people continue to improve their ability to work together and by this effort we expect to make all targets by the end of the period.

FIGURE 7.2 *Corporate OPPM*

Copyright O.C. Tanner 2009.

Rotating the page 90 degrees so that the page is top up, the reader will find the supporting one-year initiatives that are thought to be accomplishable in the next strategy deployment period. Note that, in this example, the organization is in the second three-month period of the year. Some initiatives have already been completed, some initiatives are well underway, and some initiatives are just beginning or are yet to begin.

The next quarter at the right hand side of the page presents the schedule, along with those who are responsible for leading each initiative as well as the executive leaders who will sponsor each initiative. The role of the sponsor is to:

- Provide a direct link and report between the initiative and the executive team
- Provide vision, mission and strategic direction, and understanding to the initiative leader
- Be a liaison between the initiative and the rest of the organization, providing coordination between the initiative and the organization and resource support to the initiative
- Be a *sensei* for the initiative

The final quarter of the OPPM, the bottom of the page, then presents summary and forecast information as appropriate to the particular initiative. In this example, the initiative leader and the sponsor have written a brief summary statement of the initiative and provided a cost summary (bar graph) of the initiative.

Figure 7.3 presents the corporate OPPM/A3 in which the corporate OPPM is included.

The corporate OPPM/A3 will most often be in a Scan–Plan–Do–Check–Act format. Note that the word *Scan* has been added. Before one can begin the first cycle of PDCA, it is necessary to first Scan the environment to develop a basis on which to build a plan. Subsequent cycles of PDCA will build from the previous PDCA cycle. Scanning before the first cycle is an appropriate way to start into the PDCA cycles. Figure 7.4 presents the scan summary. The leaders most likely reviewed more than is shown here, but they then determined this information to be of most importance to their OPPM/A3.

After the Scan step is completed the corporate leaders develop the plan. The Plan step will include a number of catchball sessions with the business function leaders to ensure that the Plan reflects the best thinking of everyone involved and to achieve alignment and buy-in. Figure 7.5 presents a enlarged view of the Plan step in the corporate OPPM/A3.

The final step of the plan is the creation of the OPPM, which will be the primary guiding and tracking document throughout the execution of the plan. Figure 7.6 shows the corporate OPPM as it is placed in the corporate OPPM/A3

The remainder of the OPPM/A3 is completed as the strategic period progresses and as the Check and Act

SCAN

Year End Data	Target	Actual	
Quality	99.0%	99.2%	☺
Cost	80.0%	76.3%	☺
Delivery	99.0%	99.1%	☺
Safety	>5	6	☹ ☹ ☹
Morale	>8.5	9.2	☺ ☺
Revenue	>674	697	☺ ☺

Market Share (McCormick, Robertson, & Wakefield)

SWOT Analysis

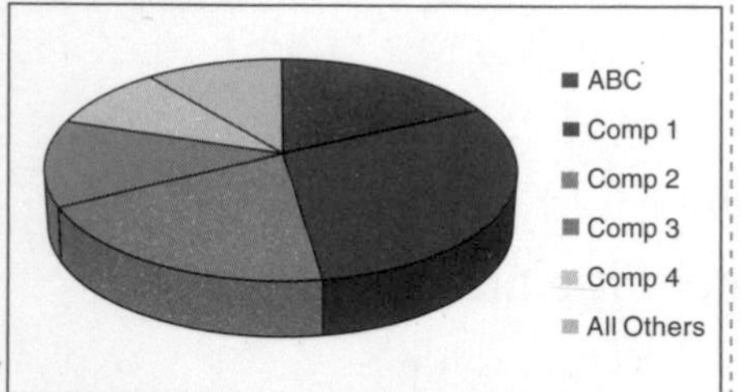

Strengths	Weaknesses
Good QEDSM Metrics 2003 No Debt Other Than for New Testing Equipment	Product Offering is Not as Broad as Competitors Operating Costs Are Increasing
Opportunities	**Threats**
Battery Chargers Uninterruptible Power Supplies Power Converters	Increasing Costs Weak Economic Outlook

2004 Expected Regulation Changes

Corporate Tax Increase 3.7%

U.L. Requirements Minor Changes
No Significant Effect

2004 Expected Cost Increases

Inflation Overall	4.1%
Copper	6.9%
Fuel	8%

Potential Supply Chain Problems/Shortages

We do not see any upcoming problems.
All suppliers have given positive forecasts.

Demand

Demand is expected to grow 3-4% due entirely to increased vehicle sales.

PLAN

Targets	2004	2005	2006
Quality	99.2%	99.3%	99.4%
Cost	75.0%	72.5%	70.0%
Delivery	99.2%	99.4%	99.6%
Safety	<4	<4	<3
Morale	>8.5	>8.6	>8.6
Revenue	>700	720	770

Increase Market Share

Our mantra, "Reduce Costs—Sell More" is becoming more important with a tightening economy and less than positive economic forecasting.

Because demand forecasts are not strong, we must increase market share. Our countermeasure will be to increase our product offering.

We will phase our entry into 3 new markets:

Battery Chargers: We will engineer this product line in 2004 and begin sales in 2005.

Uninterruptible Power Supplies: We will engineer this product line in 2005 and begin sales in 2006.

Power Converters: We will engineer this product line in 2006 and begin sales in 2007.

Reduce Costs

Taxes and Material Costs continue to increase. We will maintain market competitive labor increases, but these must be offset by cost reduction.

Our countermeasures to increased costs will be an intense focus on process step reduction and waste reduction. To minimize costs, our step and waste reductions must be done with minimal capital expenditure. All capital expenditures will be subject to serious scrutiny.

Fuel costs are a serious concern. We can reduce freight costs by moving from ferro-resonant to solid-state designs. It will still be necessary to enter into new product lines with ferro-resonant designs as these are highly trusted by our customers. But to reduce costs it will be important to introduce solid-state designs as quickly as possible. It will be important for sales to push these designs.

The move to solid-state designs will give us

FIGURE 7.3 *The Corporate OPPM/A3*

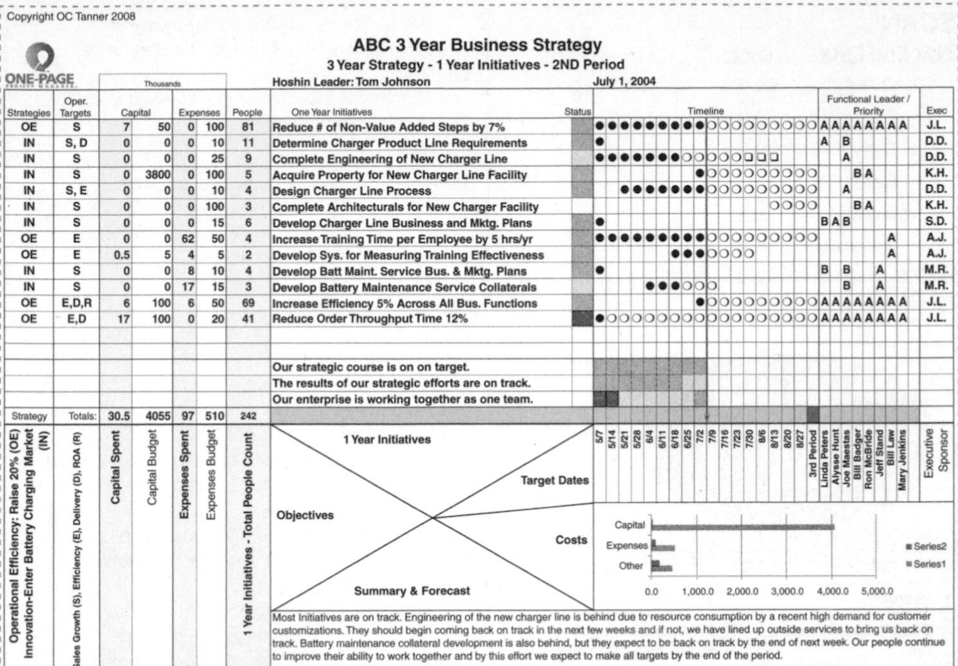

ONE-PAGE

ABC 3 Year Business Strategy

3 Year Strategy - 1 Year Initiatives - 2ND Period

Hoshin Leader: Tom Johnson July 1, 2004

Strategies	Oper. Targets	Capital (Thousands)		Expenses (Thousands)		People	One Year Initiatives	Linda Peters	Alysse Hunt	Joe Maestas	Bill Badger	Ron McBride	Jeff Stand	Bill Law	Mary Jenkins	Exec
		Capital Spent	Capital Budget	Expenses Spent	Expenses Budget	1 Year Initiatives - Total People Count		Functional Leader / Priority								Executive Sponsor
OE	S	7	50	0	100	81	Reduce # of Non-Value Added Steps by 7%	A	A	A	A	A	A	A	A	J.L.
IN	S, D	0	0	0	10	11	Determine Charger Product Line Requirements	A		B						D.D.
IN	S	0	0	0	25	9	Complete Engineering of New Charger Line			A						D.D.
IN	S	0	3800	0	100	5	Acquire Property for New Charger Line Facility				B	A				K.H.
IN	S, E	0	0	0	10	4	Design Charger Line Process			A						D.D.
IN	S	0	0	0	100	3	Complete Architecturals for New Charger Facility				B	A				K.H.
IN	S	0	0	0	15	6	Develop Charger Line Business and Mktg. Plans	B	A	B						S.D.
OE	E	0	0	62	50	4	Increase Training Time per Employee by 5 hrs/yr							A		A.J.
OE	E	0.5	5	4	5	2	Develop Sys. for Measuring Training Effectiveness							A		A.J.
IN	S	0	0	8	10	4	Develop Batt Maint. Service Bus. & Mktg. Plans	B		B			A			M.R.
IN	S	0	0	17	15	3	Develop Battery Maintenance Service Collaterals			B			A			M.R.
OE	E,D,R	6	100	6	50	69	Increase Efficiency 5% Across All Bus. Functions	A	A	A	A	A	A	A	A	J.L.
OE	E,D	17	100	0	20	41	Reduce Order Throughput Time 12%	A	A	A	A	A	A	A	A	J.L.
							Our strategic course is on on target.									
							The results of our strategic efforts are on track.									
							Our enterprise is working together as one team.									
Strategy	Totals:	30.5	4055	97	510	242										

Timeline (Target Dates):

One Year Initiatives	5/7	5/14	5/21	5/28	6/4	6/11	6/18	6/25	7/2	7/9	7/16	7/23	7/30	8/6	8/13	8/20	8/27	3rd Period
Reduce # of Non-Value Added Steps by 7%	●	●	●	●	●	●	●	●	●	○	○	○	○	○	○	○	○	○
Determine Charger Product Line Requirements	●																	
Complete Engineering of New Charger Line	●	●	●	●	●	●	●	○	○	○	○	○	❑	❑	❑			
Acquire Property for New Charger Line Facility									●	○	○	○	○	○	○	○	○	○
Design Charger Line Process			●	●	●	●	●	●	●	○	○	○	○	○	○	○	○	○
Complete Architecturals for New Charger Facility															○	○	○	○
Develop Charger Line Business and Mktg. Plans	●																	
Increase Training Time per Employee by 5 hrs/yr	●	●	●	●	●	●	●	●	●	○	○	○	○	○	○	○	○	○
Develop Sys. for Measuring Training Effectiveness							●	●	●	○	○	○	○					
Develop Batt Maint. Service Bus. & Mktg. Plans	●																	
Develop Battery Maintenance Service Collaterals					●	●	●	○	○	○								
Increase Efficiency 5% Across All Bus. Functions									●	○	○	○	○	○	○	○	○	○
Reduce Order Throughput Time 12%	●	○	○	○	○	○	○	○	○	○	○	○	○	○	○	○	○	○

Operational Efficiency: Raise 20% (OE)
Innovation-Enter Battery Charging Market (IN)

Sales Growth (S), Efficiency (E), Delivery (D), ROA (R)

1 Year Initiatives · Target Dates · Objectives · Costs · Summary & Forecast

Most Initiatives are on track. Engineering of the new charger line is behind due to resource consumption by a recent high demand for customer customizations. They should begin coming back on track in the next few weeks and if not, we have lined up outside services to bring us back on track. Battery maintenance collateral development is also behind, but they expect to be back on track by the end of next week. Our people continue to improve their ability to work together and by this effort we expect to make all targets by the end of the period.

both cost competitive advantage and cost reduction. Solid-state designs have the potential of reducing our outbound freight costs by as much as 40%.

DO:

See OPPM for Periods 1, 2, and 3
Period 2 is included with this A3
Periods 1 and 3 are on the E: drive under Strategy/2004/OPPM

STUDY:

Period 1 Review (12/17/2003) - All efforts were on track. Engineering, Marketing and Purchasing are all making good progress on the new battery charger line.

Although considerable progress has made in areas of step reduction and waste reduction, the economy continues to look weak. We must not only continue these reduction efforts, but also step up our efforts.

July 1, 2004 Update—Our efforts to reduce waste and steps continue to progress nicely. Marketing, and Engineering continue to make good progress on the new battery charger line with one exception: **Circuit board production is behind schedule.**

ADJUST:

Step and Waste Reduction Efforts must be increased. Steve will meet with each Functional Leader to determine what we can do to increase these efforts.

July 1, 2004 Update—Steve has met with the Functional Leaders and we will:

- Heighten awareness through Town Hall Meetings
- Bi-weekly reviews of our progress
- Sharing of resources where needed
- Corporate and Functional Leaders will be required to directly lead four improvements per month

Engineering feels that they can bring the circuit board design back on track. If they are not able to in the next two weeks they will subcontract the work to our board vendor.

FIGURE 7.3 *(Continued)*

SCAN

Year End Data	Target	Actual	
Quality	99.0%	99.2%	☺
Cost	80.0%	76.3%	☺
Delivery	99.0%	99.1%	☺
Safety	>5	6	☹ ☹ ☹
Morale	>8.5	9.2	☺ ☺
Revenue	>674	697	☺ ☺

Market Share (McCormick, Robertson, & Wakefield)

SWOT Analysis

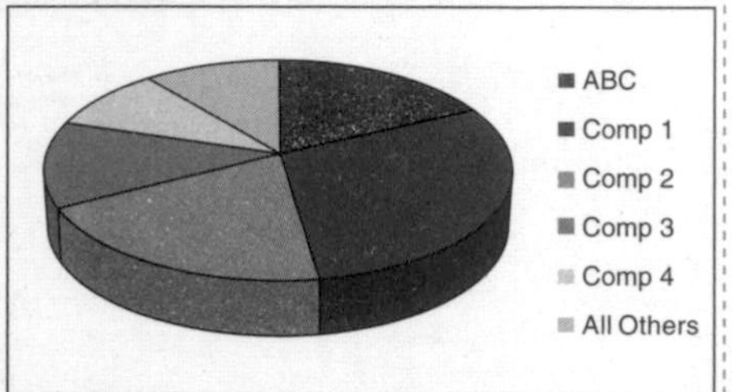

Strengths	Weaknesses
Good QEDSM Metrics 2003 No Debt Other Than for New Testing Equipment	Product Offering is Not as Broad as Competitors Operating Costs are Increasing
Opportunities	**Threats**
Battery Chargers Uninterruptible Power Supplies Power Converters	Increasing Costs Weak Economic Outlook

2004 Expected Regulation Changes

Corporate Tax Increase 3.7%

U.L. Requirements Minor Changes
No Significant Effect

2004 Expected Cost Increases

Inflation Overall	4.1%
Copper	6.9%
Fuel	8%

Potential Supply Chain Problems/Shortages

We do not see any upcoming problems.

All suppliers have given positive forecasts.

Demand

Demand is expected to grow 3-4% due entirely to increased vehicle sales.

PLAN

Targets	2004	2005	2006
Quality	99.2%	99.3%	99.4%
Cost	75.0%	72.5%	70.0%
Delivery	99.2%	99.4%	99.6%
Safety	<4	<4	<3
Morale	>8.5	>8.6	>8.6
Revenue	>700	720	770

Increase Market Share

Our mantra, "Reduce Costs—Sell More" is becoming more important with a tightening economy and less than positive economic forecasting.

Because demand forecasts are not strong, we must increase market share. Our countermeasure will be to increase our product offering.

We will phase our entry into 3 new markets:

Battery Chargers: We will engineer this product line in 2004 and begin sales in 2005.

Uninterruptible Power Supplies: We will engineer this product line in 2005 and begin sales in 2006.

Power Converters: We will engineer this product line in 2006 and begin sales in 2007.

Reduce Costs

Taxes and Material Costs continue to increase. We will maintain market competitive labor increases, but these must be offset by cost reduction.

Our countermeasures to increased costs will be an intense focus on process step reduction and waste reduction. To minimize costs, our step and waste reductions must be done with minimal capital expenditure. All capital expenditures will be subject to serious scrutiny.

Fuel costs are a serious concern. We can reduce freight costs by moving from ferro-resonant to solid-state designs. It will still be necessary to enter into new product lines with ferro-resonant designs as these are highly trusted by our customers. But to reduce costs it will be important to introduce solid-state designs as quickly as possible. It will be important for sales to push these designs.

The move to solid-state designs will give us

FIGURE 7.4 *Enlarged View of Scan Step*

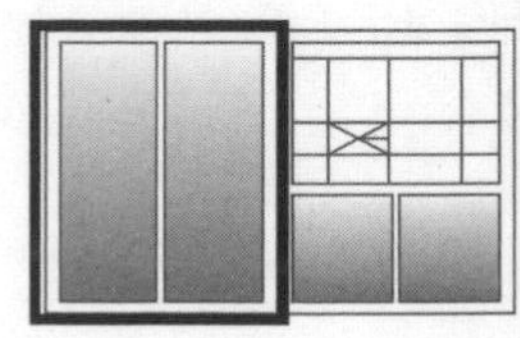

We do not see any upcoming problems.

All suppliers have given positive forecasts.

Demand

Demand is expected to grow 3-4% due entirely to increased vehicle sales.

PLAN

Targets	2004	2005	2006
Quality	99.2%	99.3%	99.4%
Cost	75.0%	72.5%	70.0%
Delivery	99.2%	99.4%	99.6%
Safety	<4	<4	<3
Morale	>8.5	>8.6	>8.6
Revenue	>700	720	770

Increase Market Share

Our mantra, "Reduce Costs—Sell More" is becoming more important with a tightening economy and less than positive economic forecasting.

Because demand forecasts are not strong, we must increase market share. Our countermeasure will be to increase our product offering.

We will phase our entry into 3 new markets:

Battery Chargers: We will engineer this product line in 2004 and begin sales in 2005.

Uninterruptible Power Supplies: We will engineer this product line in 2005 and begin sales in 2006.

Power Converters: We will engineer this product line in 2006 and begin sales in 2007.

Reduce Costs

Taxes and Material Costs continue to increase. We will maintain market competitive labor increases, but these must be offset by cost reduction.

Our countermeasures to increased costs will be an intense focus on process step reduction and waste reduction. To minimize costs, our step and waste reductions must be done with minimal capital expenditure.

All capital expenditures will be subject to serious scrutiny.

Fuel costs are a serious concern. We can reduce freight costs by moving from ferro-resonant to solid-state designs. It will still be necessary to enter into new product lines with ferro-resonant designs as these are highly trusted by our customers. But to reduce costs it will be important to introduce solid-state designs as quickly as possible. It will be important for sales to push these designs.

The move to solid-state designs will give us

ONE-PAGE

ABC 3 Year Bu

3 Year Strategy - 1 Year

Hoshin Leader: Tom Johnson

Strategies	Oper. Targets	Capital (Thousands)		Expenses (Thousands)		People	One Year Initiatives
OE	S	7	50	0	100	81	Reduce # of Non-Value Added Steps
IN	S, D	0	0	0	10	11	Determine Charger Product Line Requ
IN	S	0	0	0	25	9	Complete Engineering of New Charge
IN	S	0	3800	0	100	5	Acquire Property for New Charger Lir
IN	S, E	0	0	0	10	4	Design Charger Line Process
IN	S	0	0	0	100	3	Complete Architecturals for New Cha
IN	S	0	0	0	15	6	Develop Charger Line Business and M
OE	E	0	0	62	50	4	Increase Training Time per Employee
OE	E	0.5	5	4	5	2	Develop Sys. for Measuring Training E
IN	S	0	0	8	10	4	Develop Batt Maint. Service Bus. & MI
IN	S	0	0	17	15	3	Develop Battery Maintenance Service
OE	E,D,R	6	100	6	50	69	Increase Efficiency 5% Across All Bus
OE	E,D	17	100	0	20	41	Reduce Order Throughput Time 12%
							Our strategic course is on on target.
							The results of our strategic efforts ar
							Our enterprise is working together as
Strategy	Totals:	30.5	4055	97	510	242	
Operational Efficiency: Raise 20% (OE) Innovation-Enter Battery Charging Market (IN)	Sales Growth (S), Efficiency (E), Delivery (D), ROA (R)	Capital Spent	Capital Budget	Expenses Spent	Expenses Budget	1 Year Initiatives - Total People Count	1 Year Initiatives / Objectives / Summary & Forecast

Most Initiatives are on track. Engineering of customizations. They should begin coming b track. Battery maintenance collateral develop to improve their ability to work together and I

both cost competitive advantage and cost reduction. Solid-state designs have the potential of reducing our outbound freight costs by as much as 40%.

DO:

See OPPM for periods 1, 2, and 3

Period 2 is included with this A3

Periods 1 and 3 are on the E: drive under Strategy/2004/OPPM

STUDY:

Period 1 Review (12/17/2003)- All efforts were on track. Engineering, Marketing and Purchasing are all making good progress on the new battery charger line.

Although considerable progress has made in areas of step reduction and waste reduction, the economy continues to look weak. We must not only continue these reduction efforts, but also step up our efforts.

July 1, 2004 Update—Our efforts to reduce waste and steps continue to progress nicely. Marketing, and

FIGURE 7.5 *Enlarged View of Plan Step*

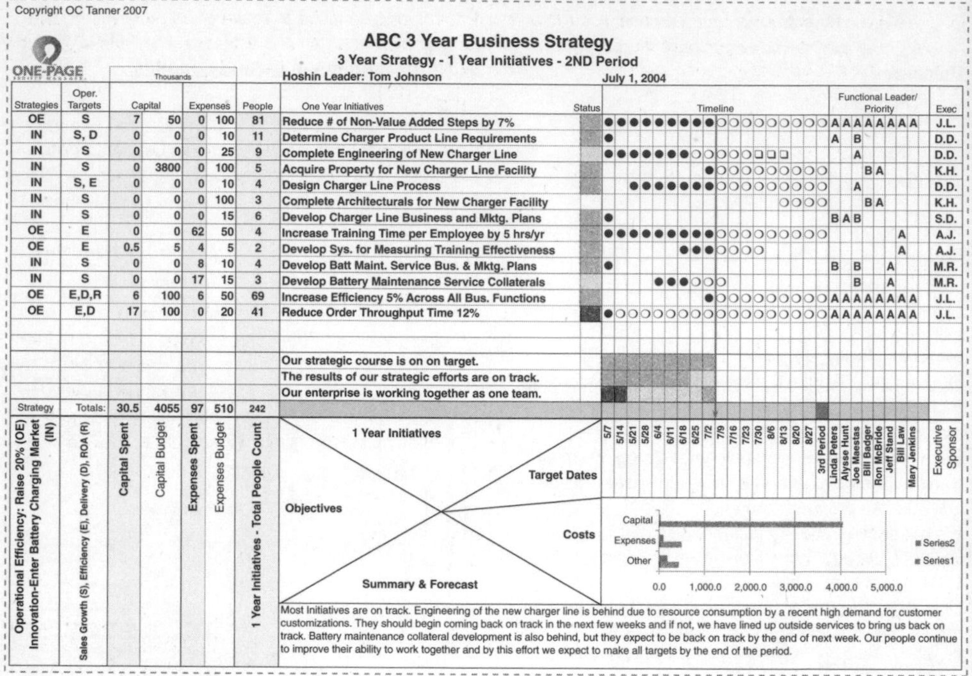

Copyright OC Tanner 2007

ONE-PAGE

ABC 3 Year Business Strategy

3 Year Strategy - 1 Year Initiatives - 2ND Period

Hoshin Leader: Tom Johnson **July 1, 2004**

Strategies	Oper. Targets	Capital (Thousands)		Expenses (Thousands)		People	One Year Initiatives	Linda Peters	Alysse Hunt	Joe Maestas	Bill Badger	Ron McBride	Jeff Stand	Bill Law	Mary Jenkins	Exec
OE	S	7	50	0	100	81	Reduce # of Non-Value Added Steps by 7%	A	A	A	A	A	A	A	A	J.L.
IN	S, D	0	0	0	10	11	Determine Charger Product Line Requirements	A		B						D.D.
IN	S	0	0	0	25	9	Complete Engineering of New Charger Line			A						D.D.
IN	S	0	3800	0	100	5	Acquire Property for New Charger Line Facility				B	A				K.H.
IN	S, E	0	0	0	10	4	Design Charger Line Process			A						D.D.
IN	S	0	0	0	100	3	Complete Architecturals for New Charger Facility				B	A				K.H.
IN	S	0	0	0	15	6	Develop Charger Line Business and Mktg. Plans	B	A	B						S.D.
OE	E	0	0	62	50	4	Increase Training Time per Employee by 5 hrs/yr							A		A.J.
OE	E	0.5	5	4	5	2	Develop Sys. for Measuring Training Effectiveness							A		A.J.
IN	S	0	0	8	10	4	Develop Batt Maint. Service Bus. & Mktg. Plans	B		B			A			M.R.
IN	S	0	0	17	15	3	Develop Battery Maintenance Service Collaterals			B			A			M.R.
OE	E,D,R	6	100	6	50	69	Increase Efficiency 5% Across All Bus. Functions	A	A	A	A	A	A	A	A	J.L.
OE	E,D	17	100	0	20	41	Reduce Order Throughput Time 12%	A	A	A	A	A	A	A	A	J.L.
							Our strategic course is on on target.									
							The results of our strategic efforts are on track.									
							Our enterprise is working together as one team.									
Strategy	Totals:	30.5	4055	97	510	242										
Operational Efficiency: Raise 20% (OE) Innovation-Enter Battery Charging Market (IN)	Sales Growth (S), Efficiency (E), Delivery (D), ROA (R)	Capital Spent	Capital Budget	Expenses Spent	Expenses Budget	1 Year Initiatives - Total People Count	1 Year Initiatives / Target Dates / Costs / Summary & Forecast / Objectives	Linda Peters	Alysse Hunt	Joe Maestas	Bill Badger	Ron McBride	Jeff Stand	Bill Law	Mary Jenkins	Executive Sponsor

Status | Timeline | Functional Leader/Priority

Target dates: 5/7, 5/14, 5/21, 5/28, 6/4, 6/11, 6/18, 6/25, 7/2, 7/9, 7/16, 7/23, 7/30, 8/6, 8/13, 8/20, 8/27, 3rd Period

Most Initiatives are on track. Engineering of the new charger line is behind due to resource consumption by a recent high demand for customer customizations. They should begin coming back on track in the next few weeks and if not, we have lined up outside services to bring us back on track. Battery maintenance collateral development is also behind, but they expect to be back on track by the end of next week. Our people continue to improve their ability to work together and by this effort we expect to make all targets by the end of the period.

FIGURE 7.6 *Corporate OPPM*

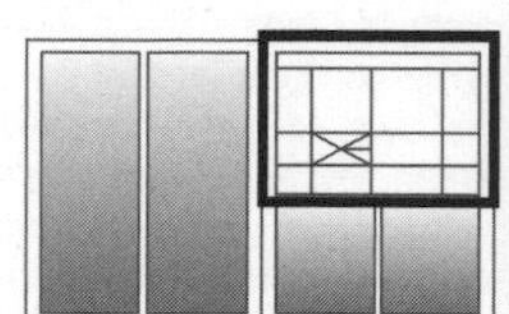

steps of the PDCA cycle occur. Figure 7.7 presents the Check and Act steps of the corporate OPPM/A3. Figure 7.7 uses the words *Study* and *Adjust* in lieu of Check and Act. These are Shewhart's words, and our people sometimes prefer to use his verbiage for the PDCA cycle.

The Corporate OPPM/A3 provides a succinct summary of the strategy and a broad-brush definition of how the strategy is to be executed.

both cost competitive advantage and cost reduction. Solid-state designs have the potential of reducing our outbound freight costs by as much as 40%.

DO:

See OPPM for periods 1, 2, and 3
Period 2 is included with this A3
Periods 1 and 3 are on the E: drive under Strategy/2004/OPPM

STUDY:

Period 1 Review (12/17/2003) - All efforts were on track. Engineering, Marketing and Purchasing are all making good progress on the new battery charger line.
Although considerable progress has made in areas of step reduction and waste reduction, the economy continues to look weak. We must not only continue these reduction efforts, but also step up our efforts.
July 1, 2004 Update—Our efforts to reduce waste and steps continue to progress nicely. Marketing, and Engineering continue to make good progress on the new battery charger line with one exception: **Circuit board production is behind schedule.**

ADJUST:

Step and Waste Reduction Efforts must be increased. Steve will meet with each Functional Leader to determine what we can do to increase these efforts.
July 1, 2004 Update—Steve has met with the Functional Leaders and we will:

- Heighten awareness through Town Hall Meetings
- Bi-weekly reviews of our progress
- Sharing of resources where needed
- Corporate and Functional Leaders will be required to directly lead four improvements per month

Engineering feels that they can bring the circuit board design back on track. If they are not able to in the next two weeks they will subcontract the work to our board vendor.

FIGURE 7.7 *Enlarged View of the Check (Study) and Act (Adjust) Steps*

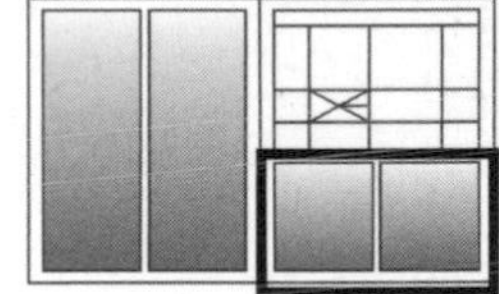

Business Function OPPM/A3

The next level of strategy planning, the second strategy deployment level, takes the broad-brush definition of how the strategy is to be executed and paints a detailed plan relative to each business function. For example, if the corporate OPPM/A3 stated a strategy for improving operational excellence, it now becomes necessary to define what that means for the engineering group, for the accounting function, for the marketing function, and for the maintenance group, and so forth.

Within this book, we will refer to this second level of strategy planning as business function OPPM/A3s to differentiate these OPPM/A3s from the corporate

OPPM/A3s. Whereas there might be only a single corporate OPPM/A3, multiple OPPM/A3s might be developed within a given business function as required for clarity and tracking. Business function OPPM/A3s are often developed for each major project or initiative within the function.

The catchball practice begins between the executive leaders of the first strategy level and the business function leaders. In this first throwing of the ball (Plan), the executive leaders make certain that they communicate clearly the objectives and their reasoning behind the objectives. They must build and establish in the minds of the business function leaders a clear vision of their direction.

The business function leaders review the plan with their people. It is important that as they do so, that they give serious thought to the plan, particularly with respect to their business function responsibility. The catchball round then continues with the business function leaders meeting with corporate leadership to discuss any problems that they foresee, any additional insights that could or should affect the plan, and a review of the business function plan and resources that will be committed in support of the corporate OPPM/A3s.

The catchball continues until all parties are in agreement. In this catchball round it is important to develop agreement among the respective groups of leaders that the second level of strategy planning fully supports the corporate strategy and that the second level OPPM/A3s are executable with regard to necessary resources being available and committed.

The OPPM format of the business function OPPM/A3s may be different from the corporate OPPM/A3s as the strategy of the organization is morphed from broad-brushed corporate initiatives to more specific and

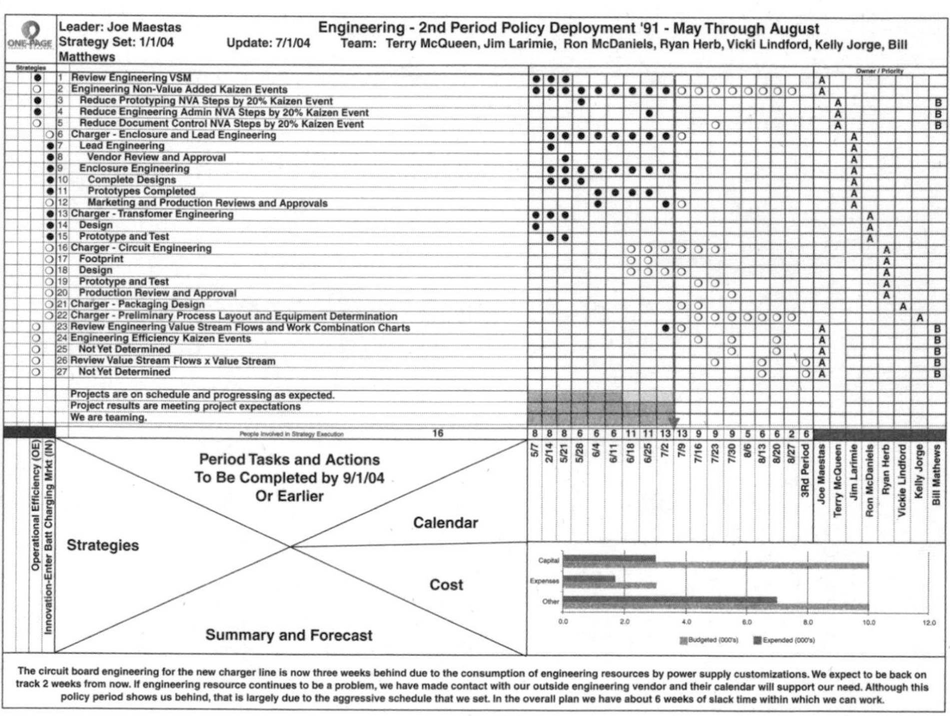

FIGURE 7.8 *Engineering OPPM (A Business Function Level Example)*

actionable projects and tasks. Figure 7.8 presents a business function summary OPPM for the engineering group responsibilities, which appear in the corporate OPPM/A3 (Figure 7.3).

The left quadrant restates the key strategies of the left quadrant of the corporate OPPM/A3. The top quadrant then states, in much greater detail, the engineering group's actions and initiatives. In the business function OPPM/A3 these actions and initiatives are planned in detail for each strategy deployment period. In this example, the period is four months and the engineering group is in the second period of the year. Again, a three- to four-month plan is about the limit of our focus. At the end of this period we will then formulate the next three- to four-month plan. Note that time periods are shortened and details are increased and made more specific to the group owning the OPPM/A3 with each strategy level.

The right quadrant can then be used to present the schedule and to schedule performance and responsibilities.

The bottom quadrant in this example presents an overall cost summary as well as overall status and a forecast of future progress. This status summary is largely qualitative and subjective. It is the leader's best assessment of the status of this group's strategic efforts.

An OPPM is included in the respective A3 for each initiative, project, or problem-solving effort. An example of the business function OPPM/A3 for the Engineering Group is given in Figure 7.9.

At the business function level, multiple formats of the A3 can be applied. In the example, we have used Scan–Plan–Do–Check–Act. The function may, however,

SCAN—Engineering's strategic efforts can be defined as being of two primary areas of focus:

Battery Charger Product Line–Current Condition:
We successfully met the challenges of the 1st policydeployment period. The designing of battery charger product is new to us and within our capability. We have some people with prior job experience in this arena. Our people are comfortable with and confident that we will complete this challenge on time.

Steps and Efficiency Improvements–Current Condition:
We've made this kind of improvement before and are getting better at it. Previous efforts haveprobably been reductions of low-hanging fruit and so this year's strategy will require a greater effort on our part.

PLAN—See the OPPM. We have carefully deter-mined which steps we will take and in what sequence. It is important that we stick to our plan both in effort and timeline. We have all agreed and committed our-selves to this effort.

DO—The OPPM gives our schedule and progress. No other notes are needed in this sub-heading at this time.

CHECK—

Battery Charger Product Line
7/1/04—All engineering efforts, with one exception, for the new line of battery chargers are on schedule. We have made good progress and all objectives are be-ing met on schedule. The designs at the point and the performance of the designs that we have seen in our simulations have exceeded our expectations. Market-ing is very pleased with the results at this point in time.Circuit engineering is behind schedule due to their resources being consumed by a number of customiza-tion requests.

Steps and Efficiency Improvements–We've made great progress in these efforts and our people seem to be getting more and more into this kind of an effort as they begin to realize the benefits of our past im-provements. The prototype group is particularly excited about their current effort to reduce steps and waste in the prototyping process. It is important to note here that they were initially very much opposed to chang-ing their process.

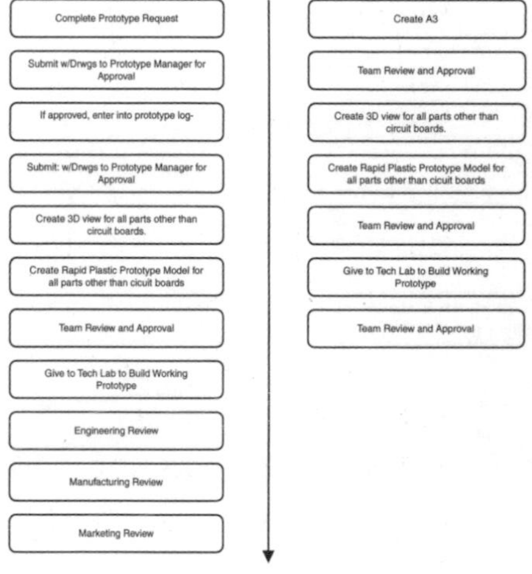

We are able to accomplish this through 2 major changes in our thinking. First, have created a special Prototyping A3. Our people feel that by adhering to the prototyping structure that we have built into the A3, we can eliminate most of the signoffs, the one exception being that if the pro-totype cost is expected to exceed budget, we must meet with our manager for approval. The second change in our thinking is with respect to the team for each prototype. In the past this has been an engineering group. Now, our teams include person-nel from marketing, purchasing, and accounting. We have seen a marked and very beneficial difference in our team discussions and we are getting through the buyoffs from these groups in one meeting.

FIGURE 7.9 *Engineering OPPM/A3 (A Business Function Level Example)*

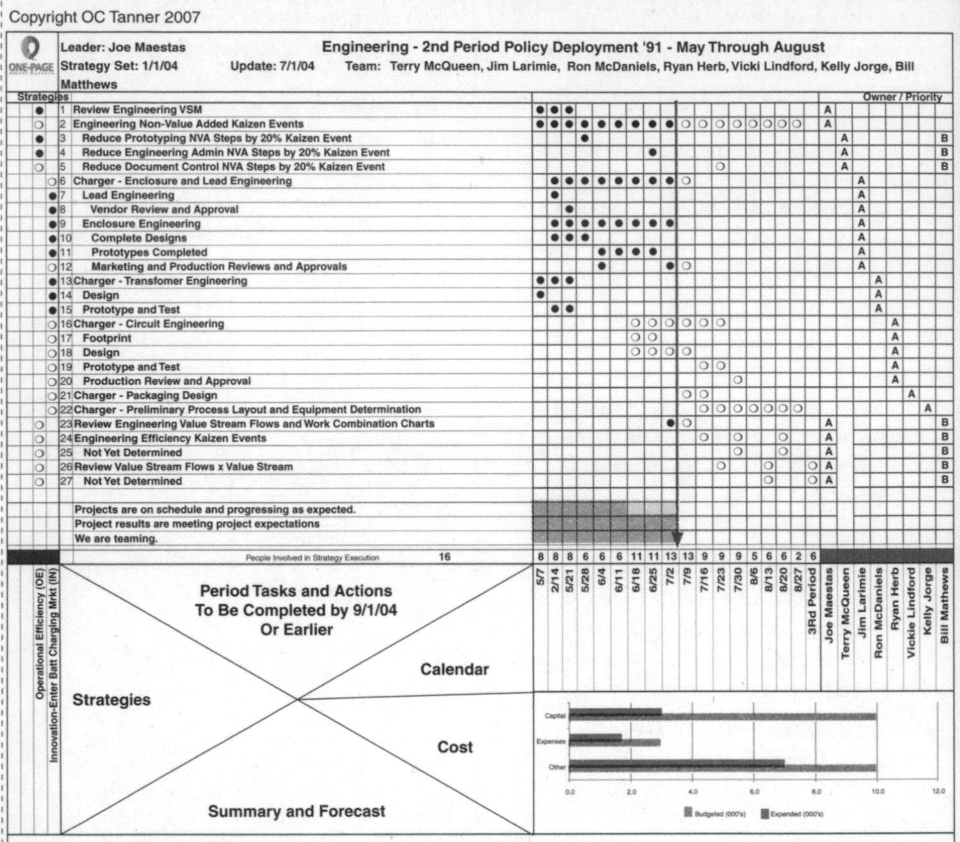

Copyright OC Tanner 2007
ONE-PAGE
Leader: Joe Maestas
Engineering - 2nd Period Policy Deployment '91 - May Through August
Strategy Set: 1/1/04
Update: 7/1/04
Team: Terry McQueen, Jim Larimie, Ron McDaniels, Ryan Herb, Vicki Lindford, Kelly Jorge, Bill Matthews
Strategies
Owner / Priority
1 Review Engineering VSM
2 Engineering Non-Value Added Kaizen Events
3 Reduce Prototyping NVA Steps by 20% Kaizen Event
4 Reduce Engineering Admin NVA Steps by 20% Kaizen Event
5 Reduce Document Control NVA Steps by 20% Kaizen Event
6 Charger - Enclosure and Lead Engineering
7 Lead Engineering
8 Vendor Review and Approval
9 Enclosure Engineering
10 Complete Designs
11 Prototypes Completed
12 Marketing and Production Reviews and Approvals
13 Charger - Transfomer Engineering
14 Design
15 Prototype and Test
16 Charger - Circuit Engineering
17 Footprint
18 Design
19 Prototype and Test
20 Production Review and Approval
21 Charger - Packaging Design
22 Charger - Preliminary Process Layout and Equipment Determination
23 Review Engineering Value Stream Flows and Work Combination Charts
24 Engineering Efficiency Kaizen Events
25 Not Yet Determined
26 Review Value Stream Flows x Value Stream
27 Not Yet Determined
Projects are on schedule and progressing as expected.
Project results are meeting project expectations
We are teaming.
People Involved in Strategy Execution 16
8 8 8 6 6 6 11 11 13 13 9 9 9 5 6 6 2 6
5/7 2/14 5/21 5/28 6/4 6/11 6/18 6/25 7/2 7/9 7/16 7/23 7/30 8/6 8/13 8/20 8/27 3Rd Period
Joe Maestas
Terry McQueen
Jim Larimie
Ron McDaniels
Ryan Herb
Vickie Lindford
Kelly Jorge
Bill Mathews
Operational Efficiency (OE)
Innovation-Enter Batt Charging Mrkt (IN)
Period Tasks and Actions To Be Completed by 9/1/04 Or Earlier
Strategies
Calendar
Cost
Summary and Forecast
Capital
Expenses
Other
0.0 2.0 4.0 6.0 8.0 10.0 12.0
Budgeted (000's)
Expended (000's)
The circuit board engineering for the new charger line is now three weeks behind due to the consumption of engineering resources by power supply customizations. We expect to be back on track 2 weeks from now. If engineering resource continues to be a problem, we have made contact with our outside engineering vendor and their calendar will support our need. Although this policy period shows us behind, that is largely due to the aggressive schedule that we set. In the overall plan we have about 6 weeks of slack time within which we can work.

ACT– Countermeasures

Battery Charger Product Line – We have given ourselves three weeks to get back on track with the schedule. If we are not able to or the moment that we see we are not going to get on schedule, we will subcontract this work to the engineering group with circuit board supplier. We have also committed to weekly updates on our progress until such time as we have this resolved.

FIGURE 7.9 (*Continued*)

have specific problem-solving efforts at the business function level, in which case the format would probably be See–Think–Experiment–Prove–Sustain.

Team OPPM/A3s

In this book, our third level of strategy deployment is the OPPM/A3s at the team or front-line level.

Once the business function OPPM/A3s have been agreed upon by the executives at the corporate level and the leaders and members of the business functions, teams are generally organized and charged with the responsibility of meeting each task or set of related tasks. A third level or a team OPPM/A3 is developed for each team. The left quadrant again states the strategic objectives set forth in the same quadrant of the corporate OPPM/A3s. The restatement of the corporate strategic objectives gives the team a clear understanding of their role in the company's strategy. The top quadrant states in detail the team tasks. See the circuit board team OPPM example in Figure 7.10.

The right quadrant designates those responsible for each task along with the schedule, measureable targets, and objectives. The bottom quadrant is used to summarize the team's progress and direction as well as any problems that need to be addressed. This team OPPM is developed through a catchball practice between team members and their team leader as well as a catchball round between the team leader and the leaders of the business function.

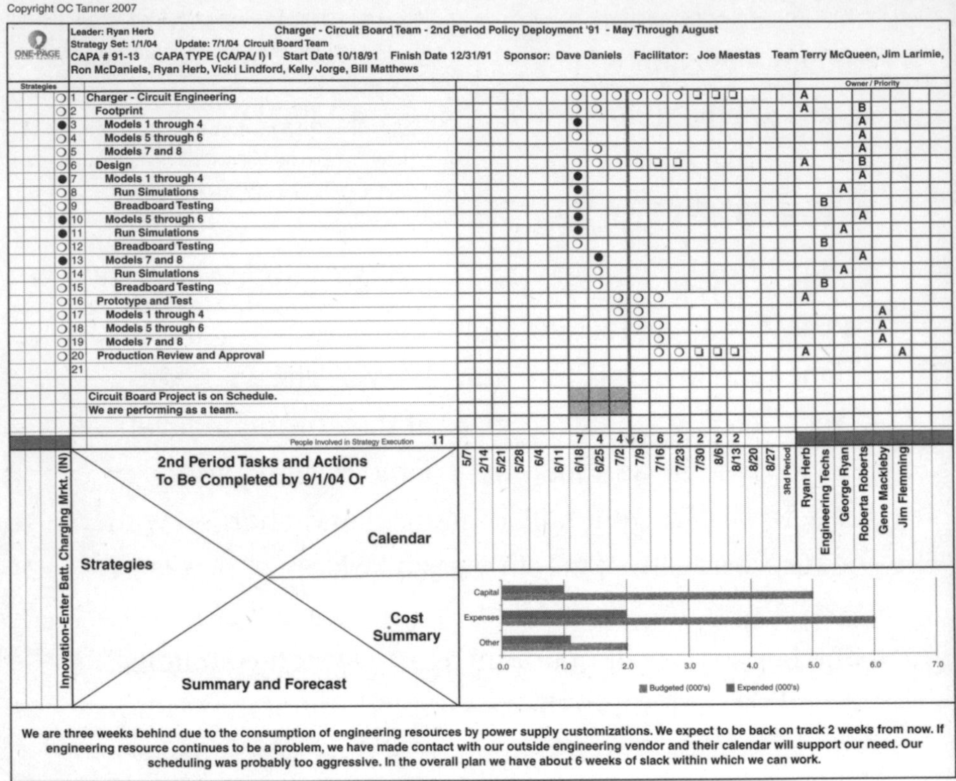

FIGURE 7.10 *Circuit Board Team OPPM (A Team Level Example)*

Each team will develop their own A3 in which the OPPM is included. See Figure 7.11. The combination of the OPPM and the A3 provides the team with a clear definition of their responsibility and their progress, and it serves also as their report to the business-function leader(s).

In the preceding example, the Check and Act information has not been completed. This is because the project is not yet complete. This information will be completed as the project progresses to completion.

SCAN: Background and History:

Battery chargers are a new product line for our company.

SCAN: Current Condition:

Although we have never engineered battery chargers, we have 3 people in engineering with strong previous charger engineering. We are fully confident that we can provide battery charging engineering that will compete with any other company. In addition to ferro-resonant experience, we can add solid state experience.

We have all required equipment and software already in place for this endeavor. The engineering costs of entering this market will be minimal. We will need additional test equipment and an environmental test chamber.

PLAN: Objective, Goal, Target Condition:

The engineering objective is to design, prototype and test 8 new battery charging models by July 23, 2004. Designs are to fully meet the requirements that we have agreed upon with marketing.

DO: Engineering

Simulations are nearly complete and all circuit problems to date have been resolved.

Marketing and production have signed off on the designs and purchasing has already given advance notice to our vendors of our upcoming requirements.

Our circuit prototyping and testing has been delayed. Resources needed for this work have been consumed by a significant increase in demand for circuit customizations of our power supply product.

We have some slack time in the schedule. If, however, the customization demand continues, we will need to subcontract this work. We have contacted our testing vendor and they are willing and ready to take this work on.

We have given ourselves a decision deadline of July 16. If we have not recovered from the customization demand by this date, we will send this work to our testing vendor.

The added cost to this project for this outside work will be about 7-8%. At this point, we believe other cost savings will offset this added cost and that project completion will be within budget.

CHECK:

ACT: Check and Act (Follow-up):

FIGURE 7.11 *Circuit Board Team OPPM/A3 (A Team Level Example)*

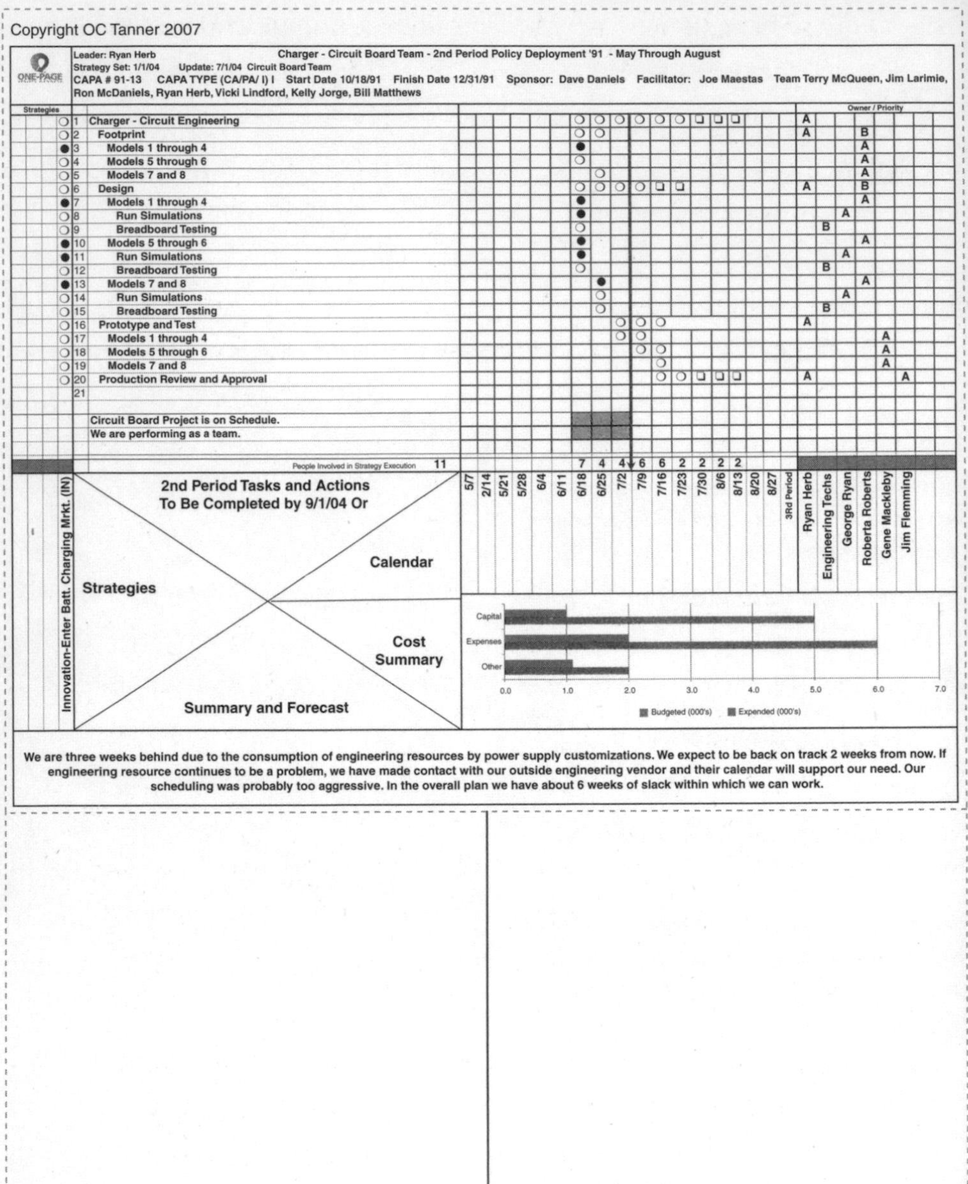

Copyright OC Tanner 2007
ONE-PAGE
Leader: Ryan Herb
Charger - Circuit Board Team - 2nd Period Policy Deployment '91 - May Through August
Strategy Set: 1/1/04 Update: 7/1/04 Circuit Board Team
CAPA # 91-13 CAPA TYPE (CA/PA/ I) I Start Date 10/18/91 Finish Date 12/31/91 Sponsor: Dave Daniels Facilitator: Joe Maestas Team Terry McQueen, Jim Larimie, Ron McDaniels, Ryan Herb, Vicki Lindford, Kelly Jorge, Bill Matthews
Strategies
Owner / Priority
1 Charger - Circuit Engineering
2 Footprint
3 Models 1 through 4
4 Models 5 through 6
5 Models 7 and 8
6 Design
7 Models 1 through 4
8 Run Simulations
9 Breadboard Testing
10 Models 5 through 6
11 Run Simulations
12 Breadboard Testing
13 Models 7 and 8
14 Run Simulations
15 Breadboard Testing
16 Prototype and Test
17 Models 1 through 4
18 Models 5 through 6
19 Models 7 and 8
20 Production Review and Approval
21
Circuit Board Project is on Schedule.
We are performing as a team.
People Involved in Strategy Execution 11
7 4 4 6 6 2 2 2 2
Innovation-Enter Batt. Charging Mrkt. (IN)
2nd Period Tasks and Actions
To Be Completed by 9/1/04 Or
Strategies
Calendar
Cost Summary
Summary and Forecast
5/7 2/14 5/21 5/28 6/4 6/11 6/18 6/25 7/2 7/9 7/16 7/23 7/30 8/6 8/13 8/20 8/27 3Rd Period
Ryan Herb
Engineering Techs
George Ryan
Roberta Roberts
Gene Mackleby
Jim Flemming
Capital
Expenses
Other
0.0 1.0 2.0 3.0 4.0 5.0 6.0 7.0
Budgeted (000's) Expended (000's)
We are three weeks behind due to the consumption of engineering resources by power supply customizations. We expect to be back on track 2 weeks from now. If engineering resource continues to be a problem, we have made contact with our outside engineering vendor and their calendar will support our need. Our scheduling was probably too aggressive. In the overall plan we have about 6 weeks of slack within which we can work.

FIGURE 7.11 (*Continued*)

Throughout the catchball practice, the OPPM/A3 is a perfect plan format for communicating the strategies, tactics, goals, and objectives in a very succinct and efficient manner. This practice develops buy-in to the strategy and its objectives at every level of the organization.

Virtually every person in the organization can be involved in the process of strategy deployment. Done properly, the creative energy of the entire organization is harnessed and focused and the efforts of all personnel are aligned to the most critical needs of the customer and the business.

Some may think that this is a great amount of work. Actually, it is less work and much more efficient than trying to push an organization's strategy through the organization. With time and practice, as with catchball, all parties become very good at developing the plans in a very expeditious manner, and the people within the organization hit the ground running in very quick order.

When people understand the practice, the executive group only needs to publish the corporate OPPM/A3, and all functions and teams respond quickly and appropriately, In this sense, strategy deployment develops a pull throughout the organization. Pushing strategy or mandating strategy is no longer necessary. The inefficiency and ineffectiveness of *push* falls by the wayside.

Once the OPPM/A3s are in place, execution begins. Throughout the execution period another very important strategy deployment occurs. It is the practice of frequent reviews of progress to plan.

With each review, questions are asked about progress. Are we on schedule? Are the objectives being met? Exceptions to schedule and plan are noted and more questions are asked. What is not working? How can the plan be improved? What are we learning? What additional resources are needed? How can we help the team to meet this plan?

The answers to these questions and others are captured in the OPPM/A3. Once again, the OPPM/A3 plays a very important role in guiding the reviews, in capturing the status of plan, and in communicating to all the progress completed. With each review, the OPPM/A3 is updated.

As the reviews occur, updated OPPM/A3s are passed to the parent plan or parent plan group. At each level, the updated OPPM/A3s are synthesized into the parent OPPM/A3. In this way, all within the organization have an up-to-date view of the execution of the strategy. As exceptions to the plan are communicated from a child level to a parent level, it the responsibility of both to find solutions to the exceptions and adjust the plan and resources as required to meet the strategic objectives.

All of those involved work with a no-fail attitude toward the accomplishment of the strategic objectives. This attitude is made possible by a change in management from push-style management to servant leadership. When everyone involved sees this management style change, the attitude of every person begins to change to one of cooperation, help, and support. Each review and the completion of each plan period is a point at which every effort is made to learn as much as possible from the experience and to find ways to develop even better plans in the future.

In this text we have used the words *corporate, business function,* and *team* to describe three levels of strategy deployment. Thomas Jackson in his text, *Hoshin Kanri for the Lean Enterprise,* describes the three levels as Hoshin team, operational team, and action team. In his book, *Implementing a Lean Management System,* he uses focus team, deployment team, and action team. These terms help us to a better understanding of the meaning and use of each strategy deployment level.

The overall strategy deployment process follows a Plan–Do–Check–Act cycle. First, we plan our strategy. Then, we execute the strategy. During the execution of the strategy and at the completion of the execution, we study the results. Next, we make adjustments, and then, we plan again. This begins the next PDCA cycle, each cycle setting the stage for the next cycle. Even within the strategy deployment PDCA cycle, we will see sub-PDCA cycles relative to tactics, projects, and other efforts. If the PDCA cycle is not very evident, then strategy deployment is not being used correctly and strategic efforts will very likely lose steam and eventually fail.

ISN'T AN OPPM/A3 SIMPLY ANOTHER REPORT FORMAT?

The A3 and the OPPM are living documents. They grow and are enhanced over time. These documents are documents that help us to manage, report, learn, make real improvement, and execute our strategy.

A quick statement of the Toyota Way 2001 is in order at this point. See the appendix and http://www.toyotatr.com/eng/toyotaway.asp for a more complete statement.

> ***1 Continuous Improvement:*** *We are never satisfied with where we are and always improve our business by putting forth our best ideas and effort.*

The OPPM/A3 guides the improvement process and sets the groundwork for future improvements. It is a tool that helps every participant to see problems clearly, to do a good job of solving problems, and to make real improvement.

> ***1.1 Challenge:*** *We form a long-term vision, meeting challenges with courage and creativity to realize our dreams.*

The OPPM/A3 helps leadership to state vision, to clearly define problems at hand and strategic objectives, and it fosters group creativity.

> ***1.2 Kaizen:*** *We improve our business operations continuously, always driving for innovation and evolution.*

The OPPM/A3 provides a standard format for the reporting of every kaizen and the format of the report itself facilitates innovation and real improvement.

1.2 Genchi Genbutsu: *We go to the source to find the facts to make correct decisions, build consensus, and achieve goals.*

The succinctness of the OPPM/A3 helps the user to stay focused on only that which is relevant to the problem or improvement. As a single sheet of paper, it is ideal for the user to carry along as he/she goes to the point of the problem to see clearly the details and facts of the situation at hand. It is equally a great communication tool that gets attention, does not bore with lengthy verbiage, and yet presents the essence of the problem or improvement.

2 Respect for people: *Toyota respects the community, its members, and its stakeholders.*

As presented earlier, one of the highest forms of respect for an individual occurs when we give a person an opportunity to grow and learn. The use of the OPPM/A3 teaches a person how to solve problems. The use of the OPPM/A3 teaches a person how to plan and effectively execute change. These are two of the most needed skills in a person's life, and these skills can greatly elevate a person's chance and opportunity to elevate one's place in life.

2.1 Respect: *We respect others, make every effort to understand each other, take responsibility and do our best to build mutual trust*

2.2 Teamwork: *We stimulate personal and professional growth, share the opportunities of* *development, and maximize individual and team performance.*

OPPM/A3s are almost always the report of a team's effort. As a team, the participants learn to work with one another, to listen to other opinions and thoughts, to participate in the creative process, and to take responsibility for the results of the team's efforts.

Present in every OPPM/A3 are the elements of the scientific method and Deming's Plan-Do-Check-Act cycle of improvement. These elements not only ensure that we make real improvements, but they also facilitate continuous improvement.

Important benefits of the OPPM/A3 include the following:

- OPPM/A3s help us to create succinct reports
- OPPM/A3s facilitate our thinking, particularly with respect to solving problems
- OPPM/A3s encourage root cause analysis
- OPPM/A3s engage people in problem solving and continuous improvement
- OPPM/A3 problem solving greatly diminishes the likelihood of a problem's reoccurrence
- OPPM/A3s encourage collaboration and objectivity
- OPPM/A3s help us to focus on hard data and vital information
- OPPM/A3s help us learn how to become good problem solvers.

CHAPTER

The Use of the OPPM/A3 in Problem Solving

The key elements of PDCA are that it is the scientific method expressed in simple words, and that it is iterative. The scientific method, which teaches us how to solve problems, and the iterative cycle of PDCA are the key elements of *continuous improvement*. PDCA, then, is a methodology of continuous improvement.

We see and recognize the pillar of respect for people in PDCA in two ways. First, as stated earlier, people solve problems. It is the innate creativity of man that is a critical asset and that needs to be advantaged to ensure our survival in today's world of accelerating change. PDCA is very powerful because it is simple and because it provides us with an excellent path for finding solutions to our problems. These elements free people to maximize the use of their creativity.

Second, the scientific method is about experimentation. We know that experimentation includes failure. In fact, when we experiment, we recognize that we may fail several times before we are successful. People, on the other hand, tend to have a great fear of failure. Yet, when we reflect on our lives we will most often find that most of our learning has occurred through our failures. Our fear of failure, then, is a great impediment to our learning and to our creativity. It may be of interest to the reader to note that little children don't have this fear and that they learn and are more creative than most adults. The fear of failure is taught to us in the way we are raised, in our educational systems, in our society, and in our business careers. Our success in today's world of accelerating change is highly dependent upon our ability to learn, which occurs mostly through failure. The antidote is experimentation. When we experiment, we implicitly accept the fact that we may fail, thereby freeing our creativity and our ability to learn.

The scientific method of PDCA in solving problems along with the inherent PDCA principles of recognizing the creativity of the individual and failure as a primary mode of learning, make it a powerful element of both pillars: continuous improvement and respect for people.

THE SCIENTIFIC METHOD AND THE OPPM/A3

The scientific method is a framework for solving problems. It consists of:

Observation: Observe the problem; measure and collect sufficient data to be able to understand and define the problem.

Hypothesis: Study the data, brainstorm, and determine a possible explanation for the problem data. For example, the unacceptable lead time of accounts receivable is due (from our observation data) to the overly cumbersome and complex software used in accounts receivable.

Prediction: If we improve the software interface and functionality of our accounts-receivable software, we will reduce the current lead time of 25 days to less than 5 days.

Experiment: Design an experiment to test the hypothesis and prove the prediction. For example, rewrite the software or parts of the software and collect data on the results. Of course, rewriting the software is an expensive experiment, especially if the desired results do not come to fruition. We can, however, rewrite a part of the software and collect data to see if we are on the right track. We could also develop on paper a series of screen facsimiles and have a user process an account payable from the paper screens to test how much time might be saved if the software were to be rewritten. We can very often experiment and test our ideas without making an actual change, and then, if the results are favorable, confirm the results by making a real change or some part of a real change.

A pragmatic statement of observation, hypothesis, prediction, and experiment is:

a. Define the question.
b. Gather data.
c. Develop a hypothesis.
d. Test the hypothesis by experimenting and collect data from the experiment. Note that experiments must be repeatable and all iterations of the experiment must be conducted in the exact same manner as the first experiment, or the resultant data will be meaningless.
e. Study the data.
f. Come to a conclusion and, if necessary, develop a new hypothesis.
g. Publish the results, and if the data supports the change, implement the change. Publishing is a vehicle for capturing learning.

There are variations of the key elements based on the practitioner and the purpose for the A3, but one will still see the backbone of the scientific method in the elements of any good A3 report.

THE OPPM/A3 AND SIX SIGMA

This brief section presents an example of the use of the OPPM/A3 in a Six Sigma project. Six Sigma is an excellent and very necessary tool in the world of problem solving. It is not necessary to apply Six Sigma to every problem because there are numerous other excellent tools for solving problems. However, when a process or system has a high degree of variation, then Six Sigma may be the best tool and approach.

It is a very natural fit to apply the OPPM/A3 to a Six Sigma project. The OPPM/A3 is designed to facilitate problem solving and Six Sigma is about problem solving. The Six Sigma approach is most often defined by the acronym DMAIC (Define –Measure–Analyze–Improve–Control). The basic format of the OPPM is:

- Background, history, or theme
- Current condition
- Objective, goal, or target condition
- Analysis
- Countermeasures or proposed actions
- Implementation plan
- Check and act

The parallel between the OPPM and Six Sigma is quite obvious. In the simplified language of STEPS (See–Think–Experiment –Prove–Sustain) that we use in our company, the parallel to DMAIC is equally obvious.

Some may argue that the specific meanings of the DMAIC terms are different than STEPS, and this is true to some degree. If this is a concern to the reader, simply use the terms in DMAIC as the principle sections of the A3. Used in this way, the use of the A3 will

- Facilitate the Six Sigma project
- Help to keep the project on track
- Communicate to all the direction and progress of the project
- Drive the project to completion and success

Figures 8.1 and 8.2 present a Six Sigma project on the OPPM/A3.

GIFT WRAP PROJECT

Figures 8.3 and 8.4 present the solution to a gift- wrapping problem with an OPPM/A3.

Note that this OPPM/A3 is in progress, and the last steps are not yet completed.

INCOMPLETE ORDERS PROJECT

Figures 8.5 and 8.6 present an OPPM/A3 used in solving a problem of incomplete orders.

The best practice for solving problems is adherence to the scientific method. The way in which the scientific method is stated varies by user. Table 8.7 presents a table comparing some of the statements.

DESCRIPTON & PRIMARY OBJECTIVE

Optimize gumming process, by reducing time in the gum oven by 50%.

SEE–BACKGROUND

Gumming is the process of covering the background, or unpolished surfaces of an emblem, with a gum-type substance. It is meant to protect these unpolished surfaces from being hit, or polished during the polishing process. The gum has to be cured in an oven before polishing, and is washed away after the final buffing. It is a non-value added process.

SEE–CURRENT CONDITION

Ovens are set at 200 degrees, and 8 minutes for optimal gum curing.

THINK–OBJECTIVES

Reduce time in the oven to at least 4 minutes (50%)

THINK–COUNTERMEASURES

Find the optimal time/temperature combination that will reduce time spent in the oven. Use Six Sigma as a tool for this improvement

EXPERIMENT–PROGRESS

We needed to determine a response. (How we measure if gum is cured). Gum is a mixture that includes water, the % of moisture loss, would become a good response.

We did a hardness test to prove that as the % moisture loss increased, the hardness/strength of the gum would increase. (*There is a positive correlation.*)

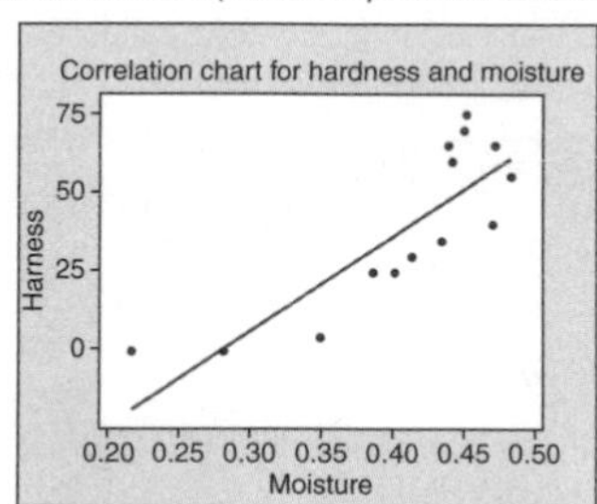

<u>% of moisture loss was calculated by</u>:

1. Finding emblem dry weight
2. Weighing the emblem after gum was applied.
3. Finding the difference (gum weight 1)
4. Weighing emblem after being in the oven
5. Subtracting that from the emblem dry wt. (gum weight 2)
6. Dividing gum wt. 2 into gum wt. 1(%) e.g:

Emblem weight		gum weight 1
After gum	dry	(difference)
0.340	0.300	0.040

Emblem weight		gum weight 2
After oven	dry	(difference)
0.325	0.300	0.025

gum weight 2 divided into gum weight 1	
% moist. Loss=	62.5%

Hardness was determined with a durometer.

We wanted to pick a range for the oven temperature and started at 400, 375, 350, 275, 260 and 250 degrees. We found these settings were to hot for the gum. The results were bubbly and flaky gum. The ovens can fluctuate 10 degrees, so we selected our highest temperature at 230 degrees. (*if we picked 240, it could vary enough to reach 250 degrees, which is our limit*).

We picked 130 degrees as our lower value, this would allow us to see a wide range.

In our **screening** experiment showed that there is not a lot of variation in the process. We tested all factors that could effect the gum process and determined that time, temperature, and emblem were all significant factors.

Factor	Type	Levels	Values
Temp	fixed	2	130, 230 (*degrees*)
Time	fixed	2	2, 8 (*minutes*)
Gum	fixed	2	New, Old
Emblem	fixed	2	Deep, Shallow

The emblem factor is beyond our control. So we decided to optimize the process, based on a time and temperature that would work for all.

Factor	Type	Levels	Values
Time	fixed	3	3, 4, 5
Temp	fixed	3	200, 220, 240
Emblem2	fixed	3	1, 2, 3 (*different depths*)

EXPERIMENT–REVIEW

Discovered that 235 degrees at 4 minutes is best

Best run: 240 degrees for 3 - 4 minutes

Worst run: 200 degrees for 3 minutes

Best predicted: 235 degrees for 4 minutes

Worst predicted: 200 degrees for 3 minutes

Center: 220 degrees for 3.5 minutes

Six Sigma testing complete.

PROVE–SUCCESS MEASURES

Gum ovens were changed too 235 degrees for 4 minutes curing time. After these changes were made, Angels and Magic had some bubbling issues. Further testing showed that the temperatures in the drawers varied from top to bottom. Sometimes in a 30–40 degree swing. The reason for this was that every oven was a built just a little bit different. Also, the design of the oven didn't encourage a consistent temperature.

FIGURE 8.1 *Left Side of the OPPM/A3 Using a Six Sigma Approach to Solving a Problem*

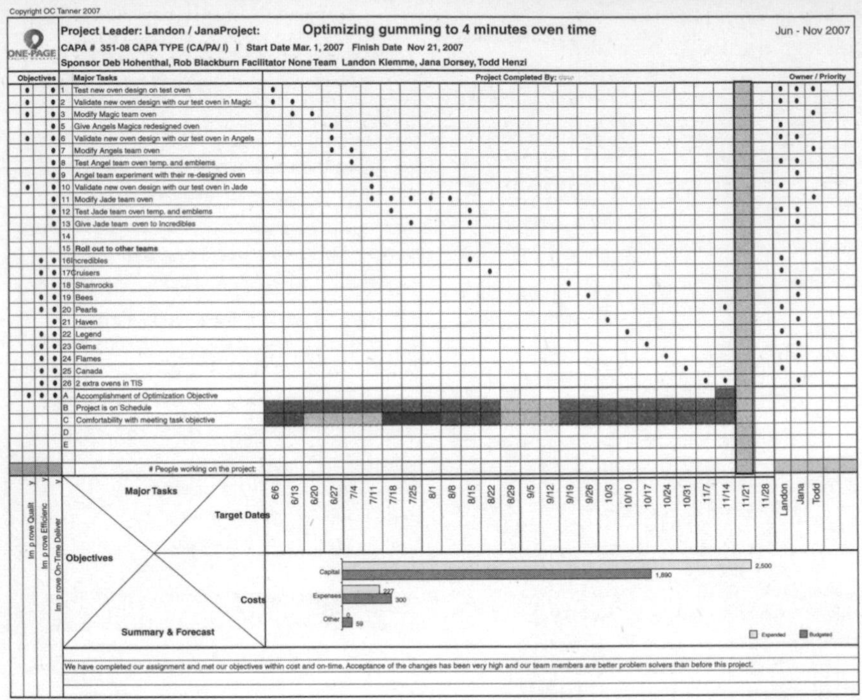

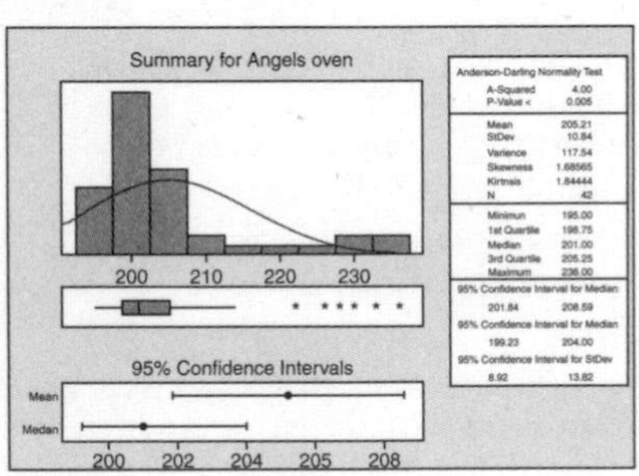

SEE–Current oven condition

Outside air brought in by side-mounted fan.

Air directed onto heating coil. Heat moves up and through 3 holes at the top

THINK–In talking with Todd Henzi. It made sense for us to close off the top holes, eliminate the outside air, and mount an internal fan.

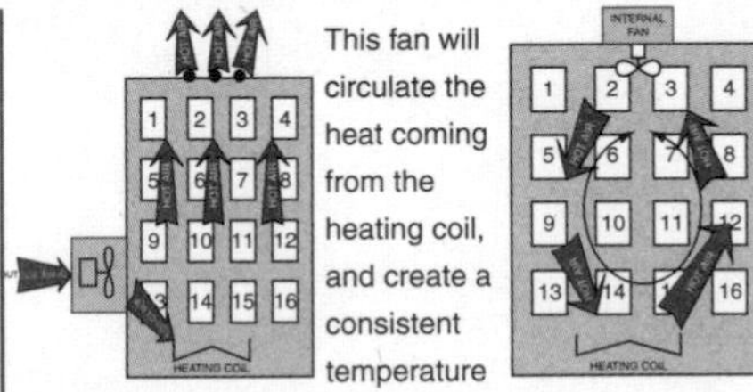

This fan will circulate the heat coming from the heating coil, and create a consistent temperature among the drawers.

EXPERIMENT–Testing the drawers did show a consistency. A difference of 5-8 degrees on AVG.

PROVE-MEASUREABLES–This new design was tested in the Angels & Magic teams for 3 weeks. No complaints were noted. Feedback was given about the consistency of the cured gum by team members in both teams.

SUSTAIN (Best Practices-Review-Migrate)–All emblematic teams have a newly redesigned oven. No other training was necessary. Objectives have been met and sustained.

FIGURE 8.2 *Right Side of an OPPM/A3 Using a Six Sigma Approach to Solving a Problem*

See–Background and Current Condition:
Currently routing gift wrap items and gift wrap orders creates many inefficiencies.
Efficiency issues are: (1) Team members doing Gift Wrap are not the same people who work the order so the understanding of an order is lacking. (2) Gift Wrap is additional routing and a place for mix-ups.

See–Objectives, Goals:
1. Eliminate the inefficiencies of the current Gift Wrap routing.
2. Research options to move the Gift Wrap process closer to or incorporate it into the Merchandise Teams.

Think–Analysis:
Team discussed positives and negatives about having Gift Wrap in teams, closer to teams, and being mobile.

In-Line Gift Wrap: Positives
1. Awards go directly to ship or consolidation
2. Over pack in Team
3. Opportunity for cross-shipping is reduced
4. Not duplicating efforts
5. Some space reduction
6. Creates flexibility (cross–training)
7. Priorities are known and acted on
8. Opens space on 1st floor
9. Improved quality

In-Line Gift Wrap: Negatives
1. Time Consuming/Team Output reduction
2. Teams have to hold inventory/supplies
3. Team needs more space
4. Learning curve
5. Need to cross train a lot of people
6. Still need to route to Cons

Plan and Countermeasures See OPPM to right.

Gift Wrap Station Closer: Positives
1. Opens space on 1st floor
2. Doesn't slow production
3. More visible
4. Less belt travel to Gift Wrap Station
5. Routing to Cons is easier

Traveling Gift Wrap Stations: Positives
1. Can be added to team quickly
2. Mobile
3. Supplies are kept at Gift Wrap Station
4. Awards go directly to Ship or Cons
5. Same as positives for In-Line Gift Wrap

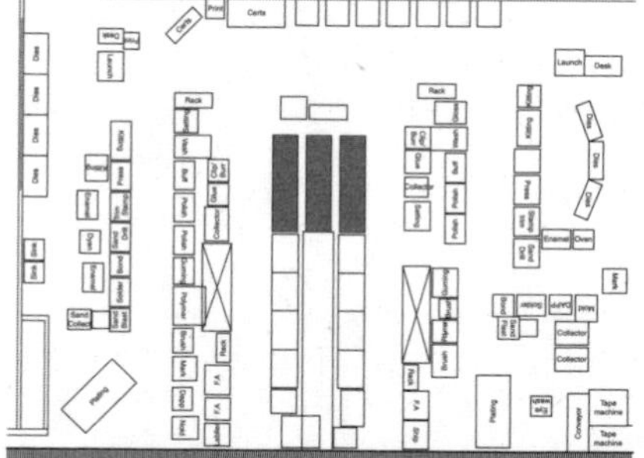

Brian created a layout of ADC 2nd floor with stations placed into the emblem teams on the north side:

Gift Wrap Station Closer: Negatives
1. Need to install diverts
2. Could become a bottleneck
3. Need to allow for space/supplies
4. A lot of unknowns
5. No quality gain

Traveling Gift Wrap Stations: Negatives
1. May not have enough stations
2. Could get in the way
3. May be too big to maneuver into teams

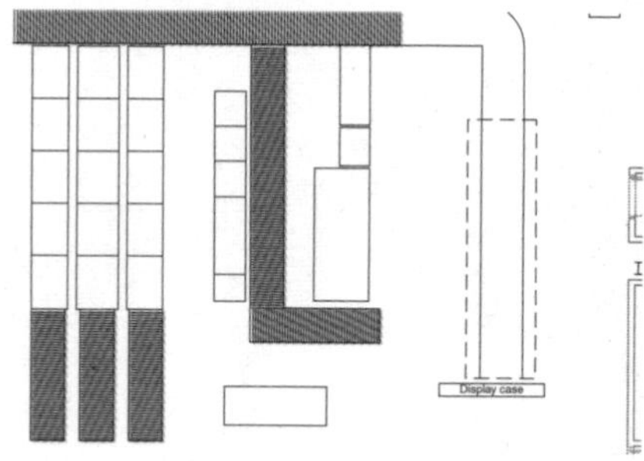

Gift Wrap station placed in front of 2nd Floor east offices 1/07/09

Think–Countermeasures
We discussed the Gift Wrap Bench design and all the supplies that were needed.
1. Gift wrap paper– 7 sizes
2. Plastic bags—6 sizes
3. Ribbon
4. Scissors/Tape etc.

Aleida collected data on how many 52" packages she gift-wraps. There were only 10 pieces in a 2-week period.
Brian created a new bench layout that would work in Janet Bill's new area.
Scott Flinders gave us a cost estimation of Brian's design. The table is 42" X 72" and has a 52" swivel holder for the large gift-wrap size.
Please notice that the table has 3 cost estimations. 1. No actuators. ($750) 2. 1 actuator, with this the table may not be stabilized as well

FIGURE 8.3 *Left Side of an OPPM/A3 for Solving a Problem with a Gift-Wrapping Station*

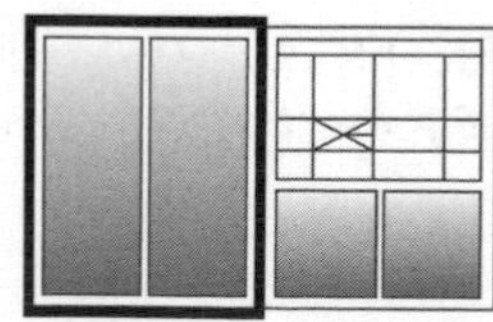

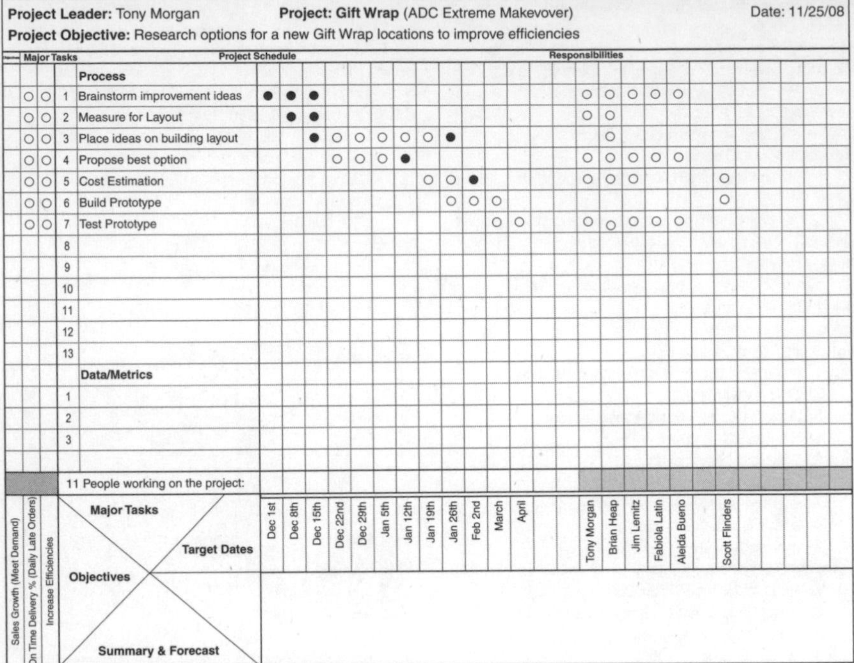

Project Leader: Tony Morgan **Project: Gift Wrap** (ADC Extreme Makevover) Date: 11/25/08

Project Objective: Research options for a new Gift Wrap locations to improve efficiencies

		#	Major Tasks	Dec 1st	Dec 8th	Dec 15th	Dec 22nd	Dec 29th	Jan 5th	Jan 12th	Jan 19th	Jan 26th	Feb 2nd	March	April	Tony Morgan	Brian Heap	Jim Lemitz	Fabiola Latin	Aleida Bueno	Scott Flinders
			Process																		
○	○	1	Brainstorm improvement ideas	●	●	●										○	○	○	○	○	
○	○	2	Measure for Layout		●	●										○	○				
○	○	3	Place ideas on building layout			●	○	○	○	○	○	●					○				
○	○	4	Propose best option				○	○	○	●						○	○	○	○	○	
○	○	5	Cost Estimation								○	○	●			○	○	○			○
○	○	6	Build Prototype									○	○	○							○
○	○	7	Test Prototype											○	○	○	○	○	○	○	
		8																			
		9																			
		10																			
		11																			
		12																			
		13																			
			Data/Metrics																		
		1																			
		2																			
		3																			

11 People working on the project:

Major Tasks / Target Dates / Objectives / Summary & Forecast

Objectives: Sales Growth (Meet Demand); On Time Delivery % (Daily Late Orders); Increase Efficiencies

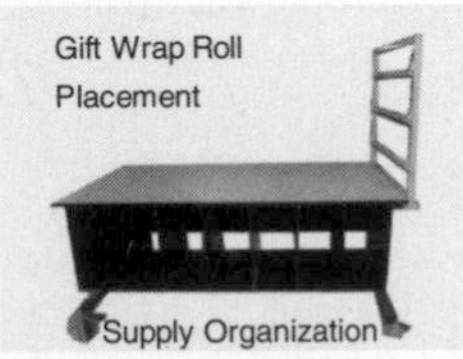

as with 2 ($1,200).

3. 2 actuators to help stabilize the up and down movement because of the weight ($1,700).

4. The add-on cost of $150 will cover the slots for supplies.

5. Jim will look at costs for a cutter to eliminate the use of scissors.

Experiment—Progress (3/13/09)

We are having a prototype bench being built that could be used within a Merchandise Team. The table is created without an actuator but could have one attached at a future time (actuator ready). The Gift Wrap table will be mobile so it can be moved easily. Approximate completion day is 3/18/09. We will test the bench to make sure team members are alright with the design.

FIGURE 8.4 *Right Side of an OPPM/A3 for Solving a Problem with a Gift-Wrapping Station*

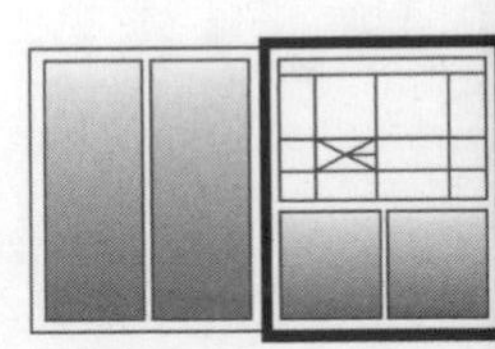

SEE—BACKGROUND

Incomplete Orders is the largest Customer Return issue that Manufacturing has.

SEE—CURRENT CONDITION:

1. The current process allows errors/mistakes to be made when gathering all components together as an award.
3. Team Members are not validating that all pieces are in place for a client's award.
4. The process is not standardized across all final assembly teams.
5. Original packaging from awards are not created to Insert additional items.

THINK—OBJECTIVES & GOALS

Reduce Incomplete Orders by 50%

THINK—ANALYSIS

1. Focus on emblems LP/Charms not being placed with award. <Created new return code for missing emblems>.
2. Understand the process and where creating an incomplete order happens. <Created a simple value stream map of the Diane's Team>.
3. Brainstorm to identify causes. <Thrown away, Not looking at lids & paperwork, and Training were the top assumptions.>
4. Brainstorm to test solutions. <On hold through December to allow facilitators and team members time to work in their respective Teams.>
5. Create Documentation to standardize the process across final assembly.
6. Train Team Members to the updated training plan.
7. Collect data on the process to validate thoughts.

There are 4 areas we are concerned about: Final Assembly, OP/Cons, the Carrier, and the Customer. These places are areas that can create an incomplete order. The Team has divided into 2 project teams to address all of these areas.

Project 1- Lori, Diane, Sharon, and Tony will tackle standardizing the final assembly processes.

Project 2- Troy, Julie, Selena, and Nermana will address the Label problems. Define what is needed and standardize.

EXPERIMENT—PROGRESS

The Team thought of piloting some ideas to try and identify the root cause.

1. Sharon's merchandise Teams will over pack all of her product that has emblems as LPs or charms. 1/23/2009
2. Fabiola's Merchandise Team will use security tape on their boxing. 1/30/2009
3. Diane's Merchandise Team will use orange poly bags to place their LP's and Charms into. (Bags on Order, here in 2 weeks)
4. The SDC will use a printed card taped to the product to alert the Customer of the Emblem being placed inside the packaging. 1/29/2009

We will pilot these ideas and watch the data to see what the results are. The Orange Poly Bags arrived 2/26/09 and we will start to use them in Diane's Team (Incredibles) and in the SDC.

The thought with the Orange Poly Bags is to make the items we are placing in the Supplier packaging more visible to the Recipient.

EXPERIMENT—REVIEW

The data being collected indicates that Sharon's Team ADC4 has not had any Incomplete Orders since she started the testing of overpacking all awards with LP's/Charms. This means that the LP/Charm is not placed inside the Supplier packaging and goes separately. It is visible as soon as the box is open. This leads me to the following preliminary assumption.

As a company we have not relayed to our Customers and Recipients the way our emblems will be packaged and arrive. Therefore our Customers/Recipients do not know that an emblem (LP/Charm) is inside of the supplier packaging for their award

A Recipient at home will open up the award without expecting the emblem inside the packaging and throw away the LP/Charm and other materials innocently as part of the packaging material.

An Administrator will set the award aside without opening the item, waiting for the anniversary event. The administrator naturally thinks the LP/Charm has not been sent because they don't know it is inside the award box (supplier packaging).

At this point the Recipient/Administrator will call to indicate that the LP/Charm is not there and request a new one. We, without questioning, (because a major portion of our Sales and Client Relations staff do not know how the LP/Charm is packaged) will create the new LP/Charm through a repair order.

When a recipient or administrator finally realizes that the LP/Charm is in the box, we have already replaced it, and they now have 2. Some return the original LP/Charm (20%) and others will keep it. The people that keep the extra emblem do so because they do not want to call and go through the process of admitting there has been a mistake or they do not want to hassle with the process of the paperwork/shipping it back.

EXPERIMENT—REVIEW

After more testing we will determine all the preferred options and costs associated with them.

After reviewing our data we have some concerns that it is not accurate. We will define and refine our metrics to make sure it is correct and reflects our true story.

PROVE—SUCCESS MEASURES 3/30/09

After months of data/testing it is proven that when we **do not** place the LP and Charms inside of the award packaging they are **visible** to the Recipient and an Administrator. We have actually eliminated the Merchandise Incomplete Orders for missing emblems by doing the following:

<u>**Old Method:**</u> Inserted LP/Charm and collateral materials right into product packaging and shipped as is.

<u>**New ADC Process:**</u>

The LP/Charm and collateral materials are placed into a poly

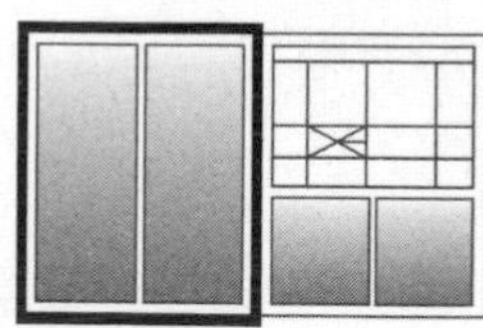

FIGURE 8.5 *Left Side of an OPPM/A3 for Solving an Incomplete Orders Problem*

Project Leader: Tony Morgan **Project: Incomplete Orders** Date: 11/03/08

Project Objective: Reduce Incomplete Orders by 50%

Major Tasks / Project Schedule

Sales Growth (Meet Demand)	On-Time Delivery% (Daily Late Orders)	Increase Efficiencies			Major Tasks	Feb 2nd	Feb 9th	Feb 16th	Feb 23rd	Mar 2nd	Mar 9th	Mar 16th	Mar 23rd	Mar 30th	April 6th	April 13th	April 20th	Apr-09	May4th
					Process														
		○		1	Research and understand Issues	●	●												
		○		2	Understand Process	●													
		○		3	Identify Root Cause	⊙	⊙	⊙	⊙	●									
		○		4	Brainstorm Improvement Ideas	●	●	●	●	●	●	●	●	●					
		○		5	Modify Training Documents	○	○	○	○	○	○	●	●						
		○		6	Train Training Team	○	○	○	○	○	○	○	○	○	○	○	○	○	○
		○		7	Train Team Members	○	○	○	○	○	○	○	○	●					
		○		8	Pilot Ideas in Different Teams	●	●	●	●	●	●	●	●	●					
		○		9	Create Best Practice				○	○	●								
		○		10	Justify Best practice					○	○	●							
		○																	
		○																	
		○																	
					Data/Metrics														
		○		1	Customer Returns														
		○		2															

Responsibilities

	Major Tasks	Tony Morgan	Lori Merritt	Diane Parrish	Sharon Armijo	Adrianna Ramirez	Nermana Kuzmanovic	Vicki Chapman	Salena Wilson	Troy Roberts	Jenny Huang	Elsa Gallegos	Shelley Watt
	Process												
1	Research and understand Issues	○	○	○	○	○	○	○	○	○			
2	Understand Process	○	○	○	○	○	○	○	○	○			
3	Identify Root Cause	○	○	○	○	○	○	○	○	○			
4	Brainstorm Improvement Ideas	○	○	○	○	○	○	○	○	○			
5	Modify Training Documents	○	○	○	○		○	○	○				
6	Train Training Team		○	○	○			○					
7	Train Team Members			○	○		○	○	○	○			
8	Pilot Ideas in Different Teams												
9	Create Best Practice	○	○	○	○	○	○	○	○	○			
10	Justify Best practice	○											
	Data/Metrics												
1	Customer Returns	○	○	○	○	○	○	○	○	○	○	○	○
2													

Major Tasks / Target Dates / Objectives / Costs / Summary & Forecast

bag and taped to the outside of the product packaging. The award is then placed into a box for overpacking.

In the **SDC** where the product is to big for an overpack box we will place the LP/Charm and collateral materials into a poly bag, tape the bag to the product inside, and stamp the packing list with the message.

Please Notice

Additional awards ENCLOSED with Product packaging.

We will then place the packing list into a packing list holder and attach it to the outside of the box.

PROVE—MEASUREABLES

The cost savings for the elimination of returns, and labor saved to not open the product packaging is $142,000 a year.

The additional costs to overpack the awards comes to $145,000 a year.

As you see the savings and costs balance themselves out.

Client Care and Operating Excellence, however, is

"Priceless"

Incomplete Order Customer Returns that have missing emblems have been eliminated. The data for the past 6 weeks indicates that the only returns received for missing merchandise emblems are from the previous process.

SUSTAIN

The process has been changed and documented. The Merchandise process trainer will train the new overpack process to all Team Members learning it for the first time. Process Audits and recertification will be headed up by the Process Owner.

We are closing this project for Merchandise Incomplete orders and will open another CAPA for Incomplete Orders that deal with Certificates, Rings and Accessories.

FIGURE 8.6 *Right Side of an OPPM/A3 for Solving an Incomplete Orders Problem*

Steps	See	Think	Experiment	Prove	Sustain
Scientific	Observation	Hypothesis	Prediction	Experiment	
DMAIC	Define	Measure	Analyze	Improve	Control
Most common	Background	Current Condition Goals/Targets	Analyze	Counter-measures	Next Steps

FIGURE 8.7 *Comparison Table of Scientific Method Terms*

The verbiage used to describe the scientific method is not as important at the scientific method itself.

It is of paramount importance that Deming's PDCA cycle be built into our problem-solving process and, more importantly, into the thinking. It is by this thinking that we place ourselves into a mode of continuous improvement. You may have noted that, at the end of the last OPPM/A3 (incomplete orders) presented, the team had already decided on a follow-up improvement based on their experience with incomplete orders of merchandise. Almost every well-executed OPPM/A3 improvement will generate additional improvement efforts.

Origins and Calculations for an A3

There is an A3 *report*, and there is an A3 *paper size*. The Toyota A3 report is written on, and named for, the A3 international paper size. Throughout Toyota, however, and in other Lean companies, A3 also refers to a management process where the A3 report itself is the central tool in a "methodology for innovating, planning, problem-solving, and building foundational structures for sharing a broader and deeper form of thinking."[1] The reason for selecting this particular paper size may have been that all necessary decision-making information needed to be presented on one piece of paper and that

[1] John Shook, *Managing to Learn*, using the A3 management process to solve problems, gain agreement, mentor, and lead (Cambridge, MA: Lean Enterprise Institute, Inc. 2008) p. 1.

the A3 was the largest size that could fit through a FAX machine.[2]

We have attempted to demonstrate how OPPM refines the A3 report and how the OPPM/A3 is a Lean tool for driving strategy and solving problems. For a "deeper dive" and more advanced A3 study, we highly recommend these two books:

1. ***Understanding A3 Thinking*** by Durward K. Sobek and Art Smalley, and
2. ***Managing to Learn*** by John Shook

The international paper size standard, ISO 216, was based on the 1922 German DIN standard 467. This standard specifies worldwide uniformity for common paper sizes and stipulates three formats, labeled Series A, Series B, and Series C. The Japanese JIS P 0138-61 standard defines the same Series A as ISO 216. The A3 paper size is defined the same way for both ISO and JIS.

The A Series includes paper sizes, based on the metric system, beginning with format A0 and then continuing with decreasing dimensions from A1 down to A10. The area of the largest size, A0, is fixed at one square meter, with a width/length ratio of $1{:}\sqrt{2}$. The mathematical principle for moving to the next smaller size is that when rectangles with width/length ratios of $1{:}\sqrt{2}$ are divided in half parallel to the shorter side, each of the two new smaller pieces will retain the original width/length ratio.

[2] Jeffrey K. Liker, *The Toyota Way* (New York, NY: McGraw-Hill 2004) p. 157

This necessary ratio of $1:\sqrt{2}$ is calculated as follows: As shown below, if a rectangle with a longer side, x, and a shorter side, y, is divided in half to obtain a smaller rectangle of longer side, y, and shorter side, x/2; and the ratio of longer to shorter sides is to be the same for both the larger and smaller rectangles, then, $x/y = y/(x/2)$ which reduces to $x = \sqrt{2}y$, meaning the longer side is $\sqrt{2}$ or 1.4142 times the shorter side.

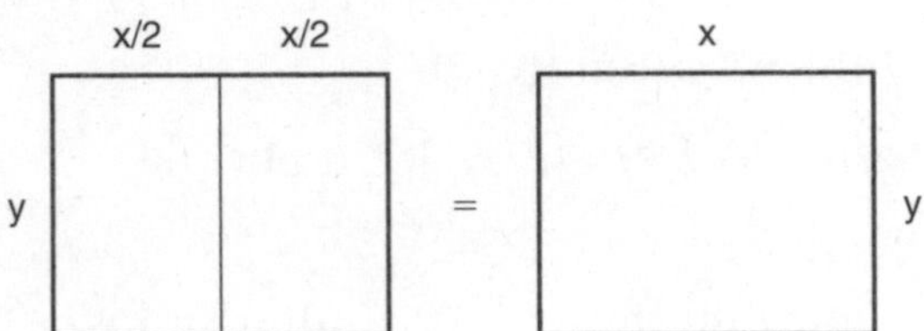

FIGURE A.1 *Equally Divided Rectangle*

If the area (x times y) of the A0 size is defined as 1 square meter (or 1,000,000 square millimeters), and the relationship between the sides is such that $x = \sqrt{2}y$, then you can calculate the length of each side of A0 by solving two equations with two unknowns. If $xy = 1{,}000{,}000$, and $x = \sqrt{2}y$, then by substitution, the short side $y = \sqrt{(1{,}000{,}000/\sqrt{2})} = 841$ mm. And the long side $x = \sqrt{2}(841) = 1189$ mm.

Most countries have adopted ISO 216. The United States and Canada have not. The U.S. "Letter" size is close to the A4, and the "Ledger" size is close to the A3. Converted to inches, an A3 is 11.7″ × 16.5.″ Therefore, most A3 reports in the United States are prepared using the 11″ × 17″ ledger size paper, which is just a little longer, and a little narrower than the international A3 paper size.

ISO 216 A Series	mm × mm
A0	841 × 1189
A1	594 × 841
A2	420 × 594
A3	297 × 420
A4	210 × 297
A5	148 × 210
A6	105 × 148
A7	74 × 105
A8	52 × 74
A9	37 × 52
A10	26 × 37

The chart to the left shows the A Series paper sizes in metric millimeter dimensions. As can be seen, A3 is A2 cut into two equal pieces. The height of A3 is equal to the width of A2, and the width of A3 is half the height of A2. These relationships continue up and down the chart. Also, the height divided by the width of all sizes is the square root of two (1.4142). As we have suggested throughout this book, pictures are often the most simple and powerful way to display complex data and ideas. To that end, Figure A.3 clearly shows the bisecting relationship of each decreasing size.

FIGURE A.2 *The A Series Dimensions*

Finally, we encourage the use of pictures and diagrams when ever possible, and we applaud simplicity. This advice from Sobek and Smalley is prudent, and aligns with our experience to, "avoid the trap of suddenly mandating A3 report writing; instead, place the emphasis on performing, improving, and learning rather than on conforming to templates, tools or procedures."[3]

[3] Durward K. Sobek II and Art Smalley, *Understanding A3 Thinking* (Boca Raton, FL: Productivity Press, 2008) p. 133

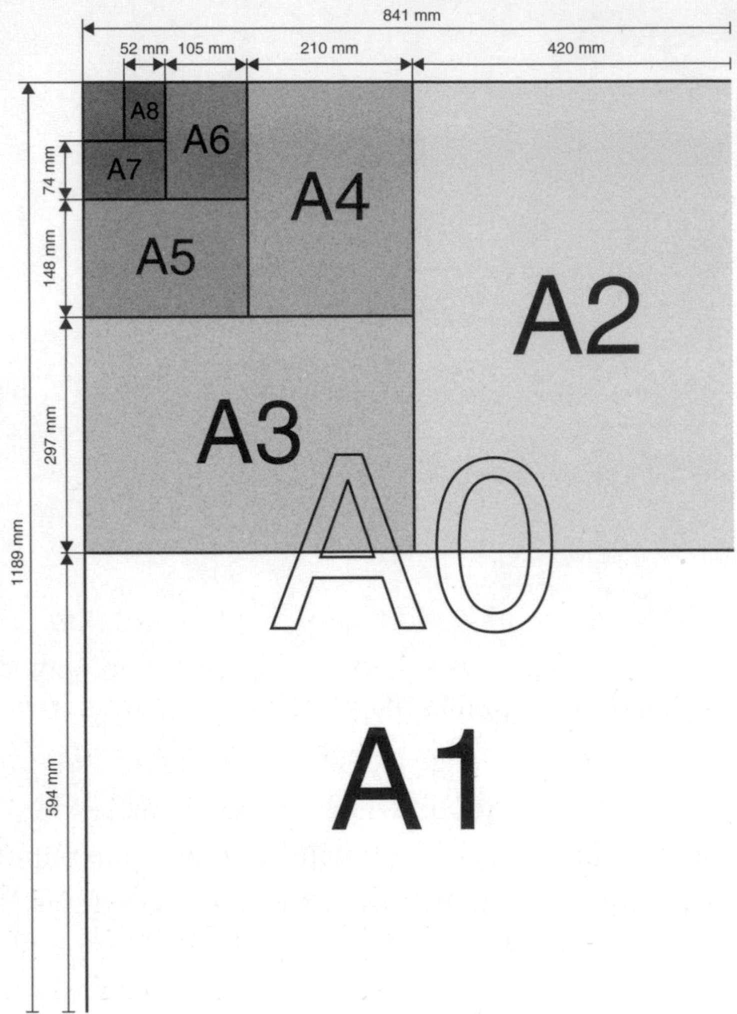

FIGURE A.3 *The "One-Page" A Series Divided*

The Toyota Business System and Lean Thinking

It is not possible to define the principles of Toyota in a few pages, and it is certainly not the intent to do so in this appendix. This appendix is written for the reader who is not familiar with the principles of the Toyota Business System, particularly those principles of most importance to the OPPM/A3. It may also provide some level of review for those readers who are somewhat familiar with these principles.

THE TOYOTA WAY 2001

For many years, Toyota has presented the principles, practices, and tools of Toyota as the Toyota Production System (TPS). The Toyota Production System provided

Toyota employees and outsiders to Toyota with a definition, framework, and basic level of understanding of the workings of Toyota. As Toyota began to build facilities in other countries, it became apparent that the TPS needed to include cultural definition or insight into the Toyota way as well as operational definition.

Why a cultural definition? Contrary to the belief of many, the TPS (Lean) requires a greater dependence on people, not less. The Toyota system is built on people, and any grouping of people brings about some form of a culture.

Crafting a definition of the culture of an organization is not an easy task. After several years of effort to provide an expanded definition, Toyota released *The Toyota Way 2001*. This document expresses the basic principles, values, beliefs, and practices of the Toyota system, which are generally referred to as The Toyota Way. The year 2001 is included in the title to indicate that this definition of The Toyota Way is a summary of their best understanding and expression of their system as of the year 2001. The use of 2001 is not so much a date of release as it is statement that the system and their understanding of their system will continue to evolve.

As with the TPS, *The Toyota Way 2001* is often described by drawing a house with two pillars. The two pillars are labeled *Continuous Improvement* and *Respect for People*. Many American companies have made great efforts to apply the practices of continuous improvement, but most have failed to give significant or serious thought to the pillar of *Respect for People*.

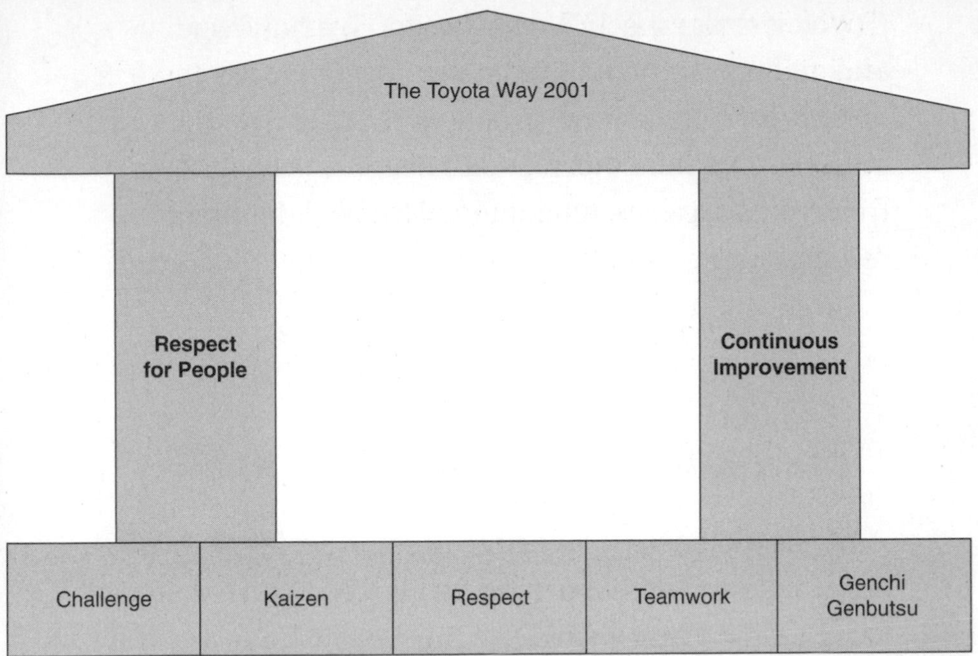

FIGURE B.1 *The Toyota House*

CONTINUOUS IMPROVEMENT AND RESPECT FOR PEOPLE

Although the two pillars are drawn as separate entities, the two pillars are highly interrelated. *Continuous Improvement* (one of the two pillars) requires a very high level of problem-solving capability. The activities of problem solving are completed by people. One of the highest levels of respect (the other of the two pillars, *Respect for People*) that we can give to anyone occurs when we take our time and make an effort to teach another person how to be a great problem-solver.

Why is this respect? When we sacrifice our own time and dedicate our efforts to the teaching of another person, we defer our needs to the needs of the other person — we raise that person's needs above our own. Deferential regard is fundamental to the definition of respect:

> *To take notice of; to regard with special attention; to regard as worthy of special consideration; hence, to care for; to heed.*
>
> Webster Dictionary, www.webster-dictionary.net

When we teach people how to solve problems, we are also saying to that person that we believe in them. We are saying that we believe they are capable and that we value their minds and their contributions.

Furthermore, people are most engaged and most satisfied when they feel they are contributing. Our greatest sense of contribution comes when we have solved a problem—when we have used our creative mind and not just our muscle. Giving our people the opportunity to solve problems demonstrates our appreciation of and respect for their talents and abilities. It demonstrates a sincere respect and appreciation of the person and the creative ability of the person.

The pillar Continuous Improvement, is incremental improvement through problem solving. The pillar, Respect for People is largely about teaching our people how to solve problems. A Toyota-like house cannot be built without both pillars, and neither pillar can fully exist without the other. The A3 and the OPPM are tools that help us to build a Toyota-like (Lean) house.

An additional benefit of teaching people how to solve problems is that we give a person one of the most needed abilities in life. Much of our success in life is related to our ability to solve problems. Those who are quick and able problem-solvers succeed. Those who are not able to solve problems fail. The same is true of companies. In today's business world, our success is very dependent upon the problem-solving capability of our people.

VISIBILITY

Access to information is an element that strongly differentiates management from nonmanagement. A domain of management is ready access to all information within the organization. On the other hand, those who are not in management have relatively little to almost no access to information. Management tends to hold organizational information rather closely for many reasons, many of which are not justifiable. Can problems be solved without information? Can problems be understood without information? Is it even possible to clearly see problems without information? No. We need information to solve our problems, information that is often restricted to all but management. Given this, it is largely only those in management who are truly in a position of being able to solve problems.

We live, however, in a world of accelerating change. The number of problems to be solved is accelerating as well. It is not possible for those few who are in management to solve all our problems, and it is, therefore, imperative that every single individual in an organization be involved in some way to some degree in our problem-solving efforts. The closer we come to harnessing the collective creative power of all those in our organization, the more competitive we become and, with time, the more able we are to dominate our industry. The starting point in harnessing the collective creative power of our people is a very open sharing and communication of all organizational information. We must make our information visible. The OPPM/A3 makes our information and our efforts very visible in a highly communicative manner.

The information that needs to be made visible is not simply performance data. We must also make very visible our strategic objectives, our competitor's data, information relative to changes in statutory requirements, marketing information, customer wins and losses and the reasons therefore, our problems, our progress in solving those problems, profits and losses, and every other item of information relative to the success of the organization. Not only must we make it readily available (visible), but we must also teach our people how to understand and use this information, thus increasing the level of visibility of this information. When we do this, we make it possible for everyone in the organization to become more involved in solving the problems of the organization. Visibility is a strong factor of true empowerment.

Much of our information consists of results. Information that is reported at the end of the month, at the end of the quarter, or less frequently is information that lacks visibility. Results that are distant from the event are somewhat like driving a car forward by looking in the rearview mirror. This information does not provide us with the visibility that we need to drive the car. We must, therefore, not only make our information readily available to all in the organization, but we must also improve the information. The information should be as real-time as possible. The closer we are to a problem in time and distance, the more readily it is solved and the better our solution. Timeliness of information equates to visibility.

GENCHI GENBUTSU

Much of our information will often come by going to the point of the problem to directly observe the problem. We go to the point of the problem to find the facts in order to make correct decisions. We also go to the point of the problem in order to develop consensus and maximize buy-in. The Japanese refer to this as *genchi genbutsu*, which could be loosely translated as "go and see for yourself." Or in other words, "Get off your rear, get out of your office, and go see for yourself what the heck is going on."

This is an important principle because information tends to be reduced and abstracted when it is reported away from its context. It is also important because, when we listen to or read information, we interpret it in accordance with our own experiences. Each person receiving the information will interpret it differently because each person's experiences are different. When we see and experience a problem firsthand, however, we each see and experience the same thing. Even then, our interpretations may vary, but not to the degree that they vary when information is not seen and experienced firsthand.

The practice of *genchi genbutsu* heightens visibility and understanding.

LEADERSHIP

Lean leadership is not command and control but hands-off and subservient. The Lean leader is a mentor, a teacher, and a guide. The Lean leader is very involved in the problem-solving and continuous-improvement efforts of the organization. The involvement is, however, quite different from what we normally associate with management.

The leader will help the team or individual structure the problem definition and the steps to solving the problem but will not become involved in the actual thinking and work of completing the steps. Even the structuring of the problem and step definition will not be given but guided through a series of skillful questions that help those working on the problem to see and think more clearly in their quest to solve the problem. A good example of this method of leadership is found in *Building Process Improvement Capacity: Structuring Problem Solving As Skill Building Exercises* (Rev. 1/03) by Steven J. Spear.

The leader will become very involved in providing the resources (support from other areas, materials, and so forth) required by the team but not within the domain of the team to acquire. When the team stumbles, comes to a roadblock or hurdle, or begins to veer off track, the Lean leader will again step in and, via a series of skillful questions (the Socratic Method), help the team to reestablish its momentum and direction.

Most of the leader's effort is a mentoring and teaching effort to develop the problem-solving ability of each person involved in finding a solution to the problem at hand. This leader may even allow those involved in the problem solution to make mistakes or to try (experiment) with ideas that the leader has already tested and found to be of no value. This, too, is done in a spirit of learning. Should the team or the individual experience a failure, the leader will again ask questions to ensure that the learning that should take place does in fact occur.

In summary, the Lean leader focuses on the success of the people for whom he/she is responsible. In the world of Lean, we believe that almost everyone comes to work wanting to do a good job. Management's job is to help them not fail. When the people do fail, the responsibility for their failure almost always rests with the processes and systems that management has put in place.

The OPPM/A3 is a great tool for clearly communicating the problems and related issues at hand. It helps team members and management to gain clear and succinct understanding of problems, proposed solutions, progress, learning, and future direction. Both tools facilitate an environment and culture of continuous learning and respect for people.

Critical Path and Earned Value Management

Two elegantly simple metrics, both rich with meaning, have been part of project management since the very beginning of the profession:

1. Critical Path Method or CPM, and
2. Earned Value Management or EVM

CRITICAL PATH

CPM was initiated by the DuPont Company in the 1950s. The objective is to calculate and communicate the shortest completion time possible for a project and highlight those critical tasks, which, if delayed, would delay the whole project.

EARNED VALUE MANAGEMENT

EVM emerged in the 1960s, when the US Department of Defense established a computation and communication approach using a set of 35 criteria. Industry has now codified EVM in the ANSI EIA 748-A standard. Calculations can be complex, but the intent is to appraise and drive improvement in project scope, schedule, and cost with the simple comparison of earned value, EV, to planned and actual performance.

Project practitioners, especially those certified as Project Management Professionals (PMP) through the Project Management Institute (PMI) are well acquainted with both CPM and EVM together with their features, requirements, formulations, and calculations, as well as their strengths and weaknesses. We have included this appendix on CPM and EVM not for the purpose of educating or advocating but to show how project managers have included these metrics in their OPPMs.

The combination of the powerfully visual nature of OPPM, augmented by showing either CPM or EVM, adds specific early warnings to the report. Over the years, project managers have shared with us various ways to accomplish this.

CRITICAL PATH SHOWN ON THE OPPM

By design, OPPM tasks do not show dependencies; therefore, a critical path is not readily apparent. Experience has shown that full PERT charts and graphical network illustrations of the Work Breakdown

Structure, though essential to project managers, tend to over-communicate and therefore don't communicate to important stakeholders.

Simple OPPM techniques, however, have been used to highlight the critical path. The easiest and clearest technique we have seen is to print the task numbers (found at the far left of each major task) in red for those major tasks on the critical path. People reading the OPPM easily see which tasks are on-time or ahead or behind schedule. Referencing the color of the task number, then shows whether it's critical and therefore whether its timeliness will impact the schedule of the project as a whole.

Powerful OPPMs should be able to be read without additional explanation. They communicate best to the broadest audience when they are intuitive and devoid of translation keys. The red numbering technique works because those who understand and request CPM data will know what to look for. For others, it does not further clutter the OPPM.

EARNED VALUE SHOWN ON THE OPPM

The basic OPPM shows a bar in the lower right section representing total project cost. Actual cost is shown with both an amount and a color indicating the seriousness of any overruns. (See How to Read the OPPM in Chapter 2.) Without the performance to schedule shown in the middle of the OPPM, the cost comparison graph is insufficient, since with that data alone, you don't know whether you are getting the value (scope and timing) you wanted for what you planned to pay.

What appears to be under budget—good—news could really be bad news with reduced spending due primarily to delayed work. Or apparent over-budget bad news could really be good news as extra expenditures have produced greater scope in less time than originally planned.

Earned Value Management is specifically designed to address these issues by simply comparing value earned with value planned.

Unfortunately, there are relatively few executives and project stakeholders who understand EVM. We recommend one delightful book that makes the complex that requirements and benefits of EVM easy and accessible, along with another that is an in-depth tutorial.

1. ***Project Management: The CommonSense Approach: Using Earned Value to Balance the Triple Constraint* (Third Edition),** by Lee R. Lambert and Erin Lambert, and
2. ***Earned Value Project Management* (Third Edition)** by Quentin Fleming, and Joel Koppelman.

Again, we will not go into the methods and essential elements necessary for EV calculations. The costs section of the OPPM in the lower right of the document is the place to show Earned Value comparisons. The most visually clear depiction of EV on an OPPM we have seen shows three stacked horizontal bars.

One represents actual cost for actual work (AC), one represents planned cost for planned work (PV), and another represents planned cost for actual work (EV).

The schedule variance is visible by comparing EV to PV. The cost variance is shown by comparing EV to AC. Finally, the EV bar is given a color—green for acceptable values, yellow for modest negative values, and red for unacceptable negative values.

As previously warned, you should be careful not to clutter your OPPM, yet some have found real value in showing the Cost Performance Index (CPI) and the Schedule Performance Index (SPI).

CPI = EV / AC and SPI = EV/PV

These are included as qualitative major tasks, and given color designations following each reporting period-green when the value is greater than one and yellow or red for predetermined values less than one.

A final word of caution. The power of the OPPM is that anyone familiar with it can immediately read it and glean the important information it contains. The simpler you make your OPPM the more successful the deployment of your project and the communication of your project's performance will be. As a successful project manager, you are, by your very nature, detailed oriented. That concentration on details has long been an important contributor to your success. You follow up on things, you readily chart, graph, and measure, and you know and understand detail—which is why you have to fight your own inclination to be complex.

Initially, it will feel counterintuitive to keep the OPPM as simple and consistent as possible, but trust us: The simpler the tool, the more successful your project will be. Add CPM or EVM only if you really use it and can efficiently obtain it, and if those to whom you communicate want it and know what it means.

Clark A. Campbell

Clark is the Founder and CEO of OPPM International and a professor (lecturer), at the David Eccles School of Business at the University of Utah. He is the award winning author of the highly acclaimed best selling OPPM™ series. *The One-Page Project Manager*, published by John Wiley & Sons, Inc. is now in its eighth printing and has been printed in six languages; *The One-Page Project Manager for IT Projects* is in its second printing. He has taught the power and simplicity of OPPM™ to graduate students at U.S. Universities and at the Tsinghua and Peking Universities in Beijing, China. He has advised corporations including GE, Zimmer, Questar, ARUP Labs, and Medtronic in the United States, Great Britain, Canada, and China. With a BS in Chemical Engineering and an MBA, Clark had planning and project management responsibilities with the DuPont Chemical Company at their headquarters in Wilmington, Delaware. He joined the University of Utah Executive Education faculty following his retirement from O.C. Tanner Company, where he had worked for 30 years, concluding as senior vice president and chief project officer. Clark and his wife Meredith (violinist and recording artist) are the parents of seven children and have ten grandchildren.

Mike Collins

Mike has been a student of the Toyota Production System (TPS) for thirty years. In the 1980s, as vice president and general manager of the American Shizuki Corporation, he managed the U.S. and Mexico operations for this electrical component manufacturer. The Shizuki Corporation is a member of the NPS (New Production System) group, which is limited to one company from each industry and focuses on utilizing and improving the Toyota Production System. His position at Shizuki initially included two years of daily tutoring under "Lean Sensei" Yasuhiko Kajikawa, currently President and CEO. After leaving Shizuki, Mike moved to Singapore and joined Worldtech, which provides business improvement consulting services to companies throughout Southeast Asia, where he was engaged in strategy deployment and developed simplified methods for solving complex business problems. Mike has been with the O.C. Tanner Company since 1997 as vice president of Lean Enterprise development. There, he has had the opportunity to refine and apply the principles and practices of Lean in a high volume, diverse environment. For the past six years, in addition to his Tanner responsibilities, Mike has been teaching operations management and Lean business practices at Westminster College.